PRENTICE HALL
WRITING AND GRAMMAR

Reading Support Practice Book

Grade Eight

PEARSON
Prentice Hall

Boston, Massachusetts,
Upper Saddle River, New Jersey

ISBN 0-13-361699-1

1 2 3 4 5 6 7 8 9 10   10 09 08 07 06

CONTENTS

NAME ________________________________ **DATE** ____________

Read the following passage. Then answer the questions that follow. Write the letter of the correct answer on the line at the right.

> Brown was at the wheel. I paused in the middle of the room, all fixed to make my bow, but Brown did not look around. I thought he took a furtive glance at me out of the corner of his eye, but as not even this notice was repeated, I judged I had been mistaken.

[Mark Twain, "Cub Pilot on the Mississippi"]

1. From context clues in the passage, how would you define *furtive*?   1. ______
   A. generous   **B.** skillful   **C.** sly   **D.** obvious

2. Which of the following words does not rhyme with *thought*?   2. ______
   A. bought   **B.** ought   **C.** caught   **D.** drought

3. How should the word *mistaken* be divided into syllables?   3. ______
   A. mis-tak-en   **B.** mist-a-ken   **C.** mi-stak-en   **D.** mis-ta-ken

Read the following passage. Then answer the questions that follow. Write the letter of the correct answer on the line at the right.

> As they walked along the narrow gravel paths, they chatted about old times, the friends they had known at college together, the latest developments in interplanetary politics. They had reached the middle of the park, under the exact center of the great blue-painted dome, when Cooper came to the point.

[Arthur C. Clarke, "The Secret"]

4. What does the prefix *inter-* mean in *interplanetary*?   4. ______
   A. not   **B.** again   **C.** between   **D.** second

5. What inference can you make about the two characters in the passage?   5. ______
   A. They have just met for the first time.
   B. They have known each other for some time.
   C. Cooper dislikes the park, but his companion feels comfortable there.
   D. Cooper is direct, polite, and honest.

6. Based on the passage, when do you think these events are taking place?   6. ______
   A. in the present   **C.** some time in the future
   B. in the distant past   **D.** in the early 1920's

NAME ____ DATE ___________

Read the following passage. Then answer the questions that follow. Write the letter of the correct answer on the line at the right.

> Unfortunately, the discovery was almost always made on a Sunday. Thus a whole day was lost before the machinery of pursuit could be set in motion. The posters offering rewards for the fugitives could not be printed until Monday. The men who made a living hunting for runaway slaves were out of reach, off in the woods with their dogs and their guns, in pursuit of four-footed game, or they were in camp meetings[1] saying their prayers with their wives and families beside them.

1. **camp meetings:** Religious meetings held outdoors or in a tent.

[Ann Petry, "Harriet Tubman: Guide to Freedom"]

7. Which statement best expresses the main idea of the passage?   7. ______
   A. The posters were usually printed on Monday.
   B. Certain men made a living from hunting down runaway slaves.
   C. Unfortunately, the discovery was almost always made on a Sunday.
   D Some of the men were in the woods, while others were at camp meetings.

8. From context clues in the passage, how would you define *fugitives*?   8. ______
   A. masters   B. valuables   C. leaders   D. people fleeing

Read the following passage. Then answer the questions that follow. Write the letter of the correct answer on the line at the right.

> There was a time when the meaning of freedom was easily understood. For an African crouched in the darkness of a tossing ship, wrists chained, men with guns standing on the decks above him, freedom was a physical thing, the ability to move away from his captors, to follow the dictates of his own heart, to listen to the voices within him that defined his values and showed him the truth of his own path.

[Walter Dean Myers, "Brown vs. Board of Education"]

9. Which word sounds exactly like the first syllable in *phys-i-cal*?   9. ______
   A. fizz   B. fuzz   C. psych   D. hiss

10. Which statement best expresses the main idea of the passage?   10. ______
    A. The slave trade robbed Africans of their freedom, both physically and spiritually.
    B. Men with guns stood on the decks of the slave ships.
    C. Africans were often kidnapped and brought to the New World against their will.
    D. It was difficult to free the slaves.

11. What does the suffix *-ty* mean in *ability*?   11. ______
    A. science   C. something written
    B. in the manner of   D. condition, quality

Read the following passage. Then answer the questions that follow. Write the letter of the correct answer on the line at the right.

> A week after the release of Valentine, 9762, there was a neat job of safe-burglary done in Richmond, Indiana, with no clue to the author. A scant eight hundred dollars was all that was secured. Two weeks after that a patented, improved, burglar-proof safe in Logansport was opened like a cheese to the tune of fifteen hundred dollars, currency; securities and silver untouched. That began to interest the rogue-catchers.[3] Then an old-fashioned bank safe in Jefferson City became active and threw out of its crater an eruption of bank-notes amounting to five thousand dollars. The losses were now high enough to bring the matter up into Ben Price's class of work. By comparing notes, a remarkable similarity in the methods of the burglaries was noticed. Ben Price investigated the scenes of the robberies….

3. **rogue-catchers:** Police.

[O. Henry, "A Retrieved Reformation"]

12. When did Ben Price become involved in these events?   12. ______
    A. before the burglary in Jefferson City
    B. after the burglary in Logansport
    C. after the burglary in Jefferson City
    D. after the release of Valentine

13. Which item below best describes the author's purpose and point of view   13. ______
    in the passage?
    A. to entertain; first person
    B. to persuade; first person
    C. to entertain; third person
    D. to describe; third person

14. Which of the following statements best summarizes the passage?   14. ______
    A. After three very similar burglaries, the losses were high enough so that
       Ben Price became involved in the investigation.
    B. Ben Price was reluctant, but he agreed to take charge of the investigation.
    C. All three burglaries involved similar methods.
    D. The manufacturers of the bank safes could not understand how the
       burglaries had been carried out.

Read the following passage. Then answer the questions that follow. Write the letter of the correct answer on the line at the right.

> Lincoln came to realize that if he wanted to attack slavery, he would have to act more boldly. A group of powerful Republican senators had been urging him to act. It was absurd, they argued, to fight the war without destroying the institution that had caused it. Slaves provided a vast pool of labor that was crucial to the South's war effort. If Lincoln freed the slaves, he could cripple the Confederacy and hasten the end of the war. If he did not free them, then the war would settle nothing. Even if the South agreed to return to the Union, it would start another war as soon as slavery was threatened again.

[Russell Freedman, "Emancipation from Lincoln: A Photobiography"]

15. Which statement below best expresses the implied main idea of the passage? **15.** ______
   A. Lincoln was opposed by a powerful group of senators.
   B. The end of slavery was a vital objective in fighting the war and bringing
       it to an end.
   C. Lincoln could not make up his mind whether or not to free the slaves.
   D. Bold action might be risky without the cooperation of Republicans in
       the Senate.

16. Which statement below best paraphrases the last sentence of the passage? **16.** ______
   A. The South would never agree to return to the Union if slavery were
       outlawed.
   B. An attack on slavery would risk prolonging the war.
   C. If slavery were not ended once and for all, there would always be a risk
       of another war over the issue.
   D. Slavery could not be outlawed if the war did not end.

17. What is the meaning of the suffix *-ly* in *boldly*? **17.** ______
   A. state, quality, degree   **C.** in the manner of
   B. action, process   **D.** the most

Read the following passage. Then answer the questions that follow. Write the letter of the correct answer on the line at the right.

> Often Andy just wandered through the woods to think or to write a poem. Sometimes he sat quietly for hours, studying animal behavior. He spotted deer and red foxes. He captured salamanders, snakes, mice, and moles; after learning all he could from observing each animal, Andy carefully carried it back to its home in the woods. The wetlands were too important to cover with concrete and steel. Andy couldn't allow Pontiacs and Toyotas to replace blue herons and shy wood turtles. He couldn't permit blaring car horns to muffle the cree of the red-tailed hawk.

[Barbara A. Lewis, "Saving the Wetlands"]

18. Which of the following states a fact in the passage?   18. ______
    A. Pontiacs and Toyotas are popular cars.
    B. Andy was a good observer of wildlife.
    C. Sometimes Andy sat quietly for hours in the woods.
    D. The wetlands were too important to cover with concrete and steel.

19. Which of the following states a nonfact in the passage?   19. ______
    A. Andy studied animal behavior.
    B. After Andy had studied each animal, he carried it back to its home
       in the woods.
    C. Blaring car horns would muffle the cree of the red-tailed hawk.
    D. Andy spotted deer and red foxes.

20. Which statement is the best generalization about Andy, based on the   20. ______
    information in the passage?
    A. Andy wanted to preserve the wetlands but did not know how to
       persuade the residents of his community.
    B. Andy loved the woods and was a careful, considerate observer of nature.
    C. Andy was afraid the wetlands would be destroyed.
    D. Andy loved the wetlands but thought their development was inevitable.

21. According to the passage, which species did Andy capture and then release?   21. ______
    A. deer and red foxes   **C.** blue herons and turtles
    B. only salamanders   **D.** snakes, mice, and moles

Read the sentence. Then answer the question that follows. Write the letter
of the correct answer on the line at the right.

> The jury wanted to select a design that would be harmonious with
> the ____ of the memorial on the Mall in Washington, D.C.

22. Choose the word that best fills the blank.   22. ______
    A. site   **B.** sight   **C.** seat   **D.** cite

Read the following passage. Then answer the questions that follow. Write
the letter of the correct answer on the line at the right.

> My plan was clear, concise, and reasonable, I think. For many years I have traveled
> in many parts of the world. In America I live in New York, or dip into Chicago
> or San Francisco. But New York is no more America than Paris is France or London
> is England. Thus I discovered that I did not know my own country.

[John Steinbeck, *Travels with Charley*]

23. Which word or phrase signals that the first sentence in the passage expresses   23. ______
    an opinion?
    A. plan   **C.** I think
    B. clear   **D.** reasonable

24. Which item below best describes the author's purpose and point of view in the   24. ______
    passage?
    A. to persuade; first person   **C.** to entertain; third person
    B. to inform; third person   **D.** to entertain; first person

Read the following passage. Then answer the questions that follow. Write the letter of the correct answer on the line at the right.

> The day Professor Herbert started talking about a project for each member of our General Science class, I was more excited than I had ever been. I wanted to have an outstanding project. I wanted it to be greater, to be more unusual than those of my classmates. I wanted to do something worthwhile, and something to make them respect me.

[Jesse Stuart, "A Ribbon for Baldy"]

25. How should the word *outstanding* be divided into syllables? 25. ______
    A. out-standing   **C.** out-stand-ing
    B. out-stan-ding   **D.** out-sta-nding

26. Which of the following statements best summarizes the passage? 26. ______
    A. I wanted to finish my project more quickly than anyone else did.
    B. I wanted to impress Professor Herbert and receive a good grade.
    C. I wanted to create an unusual, outstanding project that would inspire
        the respect of my classmates.
    D. I was excited about the project but uncertain about what topic to choose.

Read the following passage. Then answer the questions that follow. Write the letter of the correct answer on the line at the right.

> Not all leaves turn the same color. Elms, weeping willows, and the ancient gingko all grow radiant yellow, along with hickories, aspens, bottlebrush buckeyes, cottonweeds, and tall, keening poplars. Basswood turns bronze, birches bright gold. Water-loving maples put on a symphonic display of scarlets. Sumacs turn red, too, as do flowering dogwoods, black gums, and sweet gums.

[Diane Ackerman, "Why Leaves Turn Color in the Fall"]

27. How are hickories, aspens, and cottonwoods all alike? 27. ______
    A. Their colors do not appear until the late fall.
    B. They all turn radiant yellow.
    C. They are often mistaken for elms.
    D. They all turn brilliant red.

28. How are birches different from dogwoods? 28. ______
    A. Birches turn bright gold, but dogwoods turn yellow.
    B. Birches turn bright gold, but dogwoods turn red.
    C. Birches turn radiant yellow, but dogwoods turn pale yellow.
    D. Birches turn pinkish brown, but dogwoods turn yellow.

29. According to the passage, which leaves turn scarlet or red? 29. ______
    A. cottonweeds, weeping willows, and poplars
    B. oaks and elms
    C. maples, sumacs, dogwoods, black gums, and sweet gums
    D. hickories and bottlebrush buckeyes

30. Which item best describes the author's purpose in this passage?   **30.** ______
    A. to describe   **C.** to inform
    B. to entertain   **D.** to persuade

Read the following passage. Then answer the questions that follow. Write the letter of the correct answer on the line at the right.

> Sherlock Holmes and I had no difficulty in engaging a bedroom and sitting room at the Crown Inn. They were on the upper floor, and from our window we could command a view of the avenue gate, and of the inhabited wing of Stoke Moran Manor House. At dusk we saw Dr. Grimesby Roylott drive past, his huge form looming up beside the little figure of the lad who drove him. The boy had some slight difficulty in undoing the heavy iron gates, and we heard the hoarse roar of the doctor's voice and saw the fury with which he shook his clenched fists at him.

[Sir Arthur Conan Doyle, "The Adventure of the Speckled Band"]

31. When did the narrator and Sherlock Holmes catch sight of   **31.** ______
Dr. Grimesby Roylott?
    A. before they entered their room at the inn
    B. at dusk, after they had engaged their room
    C. after Dr. Roylott had passed through the iron gates
    D. just as the narrator and Holmes reached the upper floor

32. From the details in the passage, you can reliably infer that   **32.** ______
    A. Holmes and the narrator are afraid of Dr. Roylott
    B. Dr. Roylott is bad-tempered and bullies the boy
    C. the rooms at the inn are uncomfortable
    D. Holmes and the narrator are puzzled at Dr. Roylott's behavior

33. Some information in the passage above is important and some is not   **33.** ______
important. Which information is unimportant?
    A. Holmes and the narrator had a clear view of the gate.
    B. Holmes and the narrator got the rooms without any difficulty.
    C. Dr. Roylott roared angrily at the small boy.
    D. Dr. Roylott shook his clenched fists at the boy for no reason.

Read the following passage. Then answer the questions that follow. Write the letter of the correct answer on the line at the right.

> The country was wooded everywhere except at the bottom of the valley to the northward, where there was a small natural meadow, through which flowed a stream scarcely visible from the valley's rim. This open ground looked hardly larger than an ordinary dooryard, but was really several acres in extent.

[Ambrose Bierce, "A Horseman in the Sky"]

NAME ____   DATE _______________

34. The word *visible* contains the Latin root *vis* (*vid*). What item below best   34. _______
defines the meaning of *visible*?
A. able to be touched   C. able to be seen
B. able to be visited   D. able to be understood

35. From context clues in the passage, what item below is the best definition   35. _______
for *extent*?
A. quality   C. depth
B. height   D. size or area

Use this bar graph to answer the following questions.

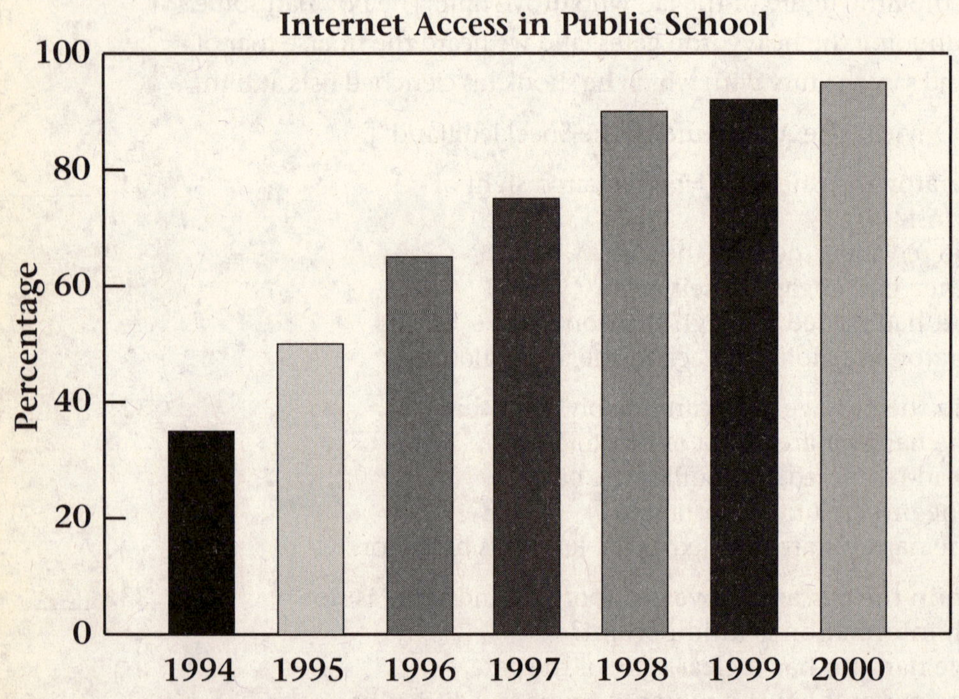

36. According to the graph, when did the percentage of schools with Internet   36. _______
access reach 90%?
A. 1995   B. 1997   C. 1998   D. 1999

37. Between 1995 and 1998, how much did the percentage of schools with   37. _______
Internet access rise?
A. from 50% to 90%   C. from 40% to 80%
B. from 60% to 70%   D. from 80% to 90%

Read the following passage. Then answer the questions that follow. Write the letter of the correct answer on the line at the right.

> Not far away, the radio operator of the *Californian* had gone to bed for the night and turned off his radio. Several officers and crewmen on the deck of the *Californian* saw rockets in the distance and reported them to their captain. The captain told them to try to contact the ship with a Morse lamp. But they received no answer to their flashed calls. No one thought to wake up the radio operator.

[Robert D. Ballard, "Exploring the *Titanic*"]

38. In which word is the *gh* letter combination pronounced differently from the way it is pronounced in *night*?   **38.** ______
    A. fight   **B.** brought   **C.** cough   **D.** knight

39. The word *operator* in the selection contains the Latin root *opus*, meaning "work." Which item best defines the meaning of the word *operator*?   **39.** ______
    A. someone who works   **C.** a person who works a machine
    B. an efficient person   **D.** someone devoted to working

40. Which conclusion below can you draw from the passage?   **40.** ______
    A. The crewmen on the *Californian* were lazy.
    B. If the crewmen had awakened the radio operator, the results might have been different.
    C. The captain of the *Californian* did not care about the *Titanic*.
    D. The *Californian* was too far away to rescue the *Titanic*.

Read the following passage. Then answer the questions that follow. Write the letter of the correct answer on the line at the right.

> Most of these immigrants were poor. Somehow they managed to scrape together enough money to pay for their passage to America. Many immigrant families arrived penniless. Others had to make the journey in stages. Often the father came first, found work, and sent for his family later.
>
>   Immigrants usually crossed the Atlantic as steerage passengers. Reached by steep, slippery stairways, the steerage lay deep down in the hold of the ship. It was occupied by passengers paying the lowest fare.

[Russell Freedman, "Immigrant Kids"]

41. Which of the following statements best expresses the main idea of the passage?   **41.** ______
    A. Immigrants often came across the Atlantic.
    B. Passengers who wanted to pay the lowest fare traveled in steerage.
    C. Immigrants sometimes made the journey to America in stages.
    D. Most of the immigrants were poor.

NAME ____ DATE _______________

42. Some information in the passage is important and some is not important.   42. ______
    Which information is unimportant?
    A. Immigrants often had to scrape together the fare to make the journey
       to America.
    B. Steerage was reached by steep, slippery stairways.
    C. People in steerage paid the lowest fate.
    D. Fathers sometimes came to America first in order to find work and then
       sent for their families later.

Read the following passage. Then answer the questions that follow. Write the letter
of the correct answer on the line at the right.

> With Franklin dead, Eleanor Roosevelt might have dropped out of the public eye,
> might have been remembered in the history books only as a footnote to the
> president's program of social reforms. Instead she found new strengths within
> herself, new ways to live a useful, interesting life—and to help others. Now,
> moreover, her successes were her own, not the result of being the president's wife.

[William Jay Jacobs, "Eleanor Roosevelt"]

43. Which sentence below is the best paraphrase of the first sentence in the   43. ______
    passage?
    A. Eleanor was tempted to drop out of sight after her husband's death.
    B. Eleanor could have dropped out of sight after the president's death and
       been remembered only as his helper.
    C. After the president's death, Eleanor Roosevelt increased her schedule
       of public activities.
    D. In mourning for the president, Eleanor Roosevelt was not often in
       the public eye after the president's death.

44. On the basis of the passage, what generalization can you make about   44. ______
    Eleanor Roosevelt?
    A. Eleanor Roosevelt was a shy but determined woman.
    B. Eleanor Roosevelt was independent and devoted to helping others.
    C. Eleanor Roosevelt was not used to being successful on her own.
    D. Eleanor Roosevelt earned only a minor place in history books.

DECODING: TRICKY LETTER COMBINATIONS

Introduction

When you come across unfamiliar words in your reading, try pronouncing the words. Think about the way each sound is spelled. Notice any unusual spellings. You may find that some of the words do not sound the way they are spelled.

Note the difference between the spelling and pronunciation of the word *taught*. The letters *g* and *h* are silent. Think about other words you know that are similar in spelling to *taught*.

Suppose a passage that you are reading contains the word *haughty*. You can use what you know about the *augh* letter combination in other words to figure out how to pronounce *haughty*, which means "proud."

In words with the letter combinations *igh* and *ought, gh* is also silent, as it is in the *augh* combination. Study the examples below. (Notice that the vowel sounds in words with the ought combination sometimes differ.)

Words with the *igh* combination	Words with the *ought* combination
night	fought
tight	drought
sigh	thought

Now consider the difference between the spelling and pronunciation of the word *should*. In the *ould* combination, the *l* is silent. Think about other words you know that are similar in spelling to *should*.

Reading Tip

Many English words do not sound the way they are spelled. Use what you already know about words with tricky letter combinations to help you figure out the pronunciations of words that have similar combinations.

Practice

Read the following passage from "Choice: A Tribute to Dr. Martin Luther King, Jr." by Alice Walker.

> At the moment I saw his resistance I knew I would never be able to live in this country without resisting everything that sought to disinherit me, and I would never be forced away from the land of my birth without a fight. He was The One, The Hero, The One Fearless Person for whom we had waited. I hadn't even realized before that we *had* been waiting for Martin Luther King, Jr., but we had. And I knew it for sure when my mother added his name to the list of people she prayed for every night.

A. Identify words in the passage that have the letter combinations shown below. Write the words below each heading. Say each word aloud. Then, write its meaning next to it. If necessary, look it up in the dictionary.

igh	*ought*	*ould*

B. Challenge!
In the *ough* combination at the end of words, the *gh* can be silent, or it can have the /f/ sound. Write at least one example of each case below.

1. *ough,* in which *gh* is silent_______________________________________

2. *ough,* in which *gh* has the /f/ sound _______________________________

DECODING: SOUND/LETTER PATTERNS

Introduction

As you explore meaning and pronunciation in your reading, you may
have noticed that certain letter patterns produce specific sounds. For
example, in the *tion* pattern at the end of a word, *ti* has the sound /sh/,
as in *friction* and *correction*.

Words that end with the /shən/ sound are usually spelled with the *-tion*
ending. In some cases, this sound can be spelled *-sion*, as in *tension* and
propulsion, usually when a consonant comes before the /shən/ ending.

Most words that end in a vowel plus *sion* have the /zhən/ sound, as in
decision and *vision*.

You may have also noticed in your reading that words with more than
one syllable whose last, unaccented syllable ends in *-ar, -er,* or *-or* have
the same ending sound, /ər/. Examples are *hangar, offer,* and *monitor*. The
/ər/ sound does not change when *-s, -ed,* and *-ing* are added to a base
word that ends in *-ar, -er,* and *-or*, as in *hangars, offered,* and *monitoring.*

Another pattern you may have noticed is the /f/ sound produced by *ph*
in words you read. The sound /f/ can be produced by the letter pattern
ph at the beginning, in the middle, and at the end of words. Note the
examples below.
- /f/ sound made by *ph* pattern at the beginning of a word:
  photograph, phrase, physician
- /f/ sound made by *ph* pattern in the middle of a word:
  gopher, emphasize, telephone
- /f/ sound made by *ph* pattern at the end of a word:
  graph, hieroglyph

Reading Tip

When you discover an unfamiliar word in your reading, first try pronouncing the word. Think about the way each sound is spelled. Look for
sound/letter patterns that you are familiar with, such as *tion/sion, ar/er/or,*
and *ph*. Apply what you already know about sound/letter patterns to the
new word. Once you are able to pronounce the word, you may discover
that you are familiar with it—even though it may have seemed unfamiliar when you first saw it.

NAME _______________________________   **DATE** _____________

Practice

Read the following passage from "The Day I Got Lost" by Isaac Bashevis Singer.

I tried to call a number of friends (those whose telephone numbers I happened to think of), but wherever I called, I got the same reply: "They've gone to a party at Professor Shlemiel's."

As I stood in the street wondering what to do, it began to rain. "Where's my umbrella?" I said to myself. And I knew the answer at once. I'd left it—somewhere. I got under a nearby canopy. It was now raining cats and dogs. All day it had been sunny and warm, but now that I was lost and my umbrella was lost, it had to storm. And it looked as if it would go on for the rest of the night.

To distract myself, I began to ponder the ancient philosophical problem. A mother chicken lays an egg, I thought to myself, and when it hatches, there is a chicken. That's how it has always been. Every chicken comes from an egg and every egg comes from a chicken. But was there a chicken first? Or an egg first? No philosopher has ever been able to solve this eternal question. Just the same, there must be an answer. Perhaps I, Shlemiel, am destined to stumble on it.

Words that end with *sion/tion* (can include *s* ending)	Words that have *ar/er/or* as the second, unaccented, syllable (can include *s ed*, and *ing* endings)	Words in which *ph* stands for the /f/ sound

Identify words in the passage that have the sound/letter patterns shown below. Write the words below each heading.

Pronounce each word aloud. Which of these words do you use in your everyday speech? What is the meaning of these words?

____

____

DECODING: SYLLABIFICATION

Introduction

A **syllable** is a unit of language: It can be a word or part of a word. Each syllable in a word has one vowel sound. As you explore word pronunciation and meaning during your reading, it is sometimes helpful to divide a word into its syllables.

Often, one or more of the syllables is an important clue to meaning. In addition, when you say the word aloud, you may realize that it's one you already use in your everyday speech—and you may not have recognized it by just seeing it on the page. To divide a word into syllables, first listen for the vowel sounds.

Pronounce the words *beat* and *create*. Notice that in *beat*, the letters *e* and *a* together have one vowel sound and one syllable. In *create*, the letters *e* and *a* make two different vowel sounds. *Create* has two syllables: cre ate.

Use these rules to help you divide words into syllables:

1. If a word has two vowel sounds between two consonant letters, divide the word between the two vowels.

    ruin   ru in
    trial   tri al
    react   re act

2. If a word has two consonants between two vowels, divide the word between the two consonants.

    injure   in jure
    letter   let ter
    import   im port

3. If a word has two of the same consonants next to each other, divide the word between the two consonants.

    common   com mon
    effect   ef fect
    approve   ap prove

4. If a word has a middle consonant between two vowels, listen for the accented syllable in the word. The middle consonant is part of the accented syllable.

    pretend   pre tend'
    melon   mel' on
    salute   sa lute'

Reading Tip

Remember to listen for the vowel sounds when you divide a word into syllables.

NAME _______________________________________ **DATE** _____________

Practice

Read the following passage from "Tears of Autumn" by Yoshiko Uchida.

> A man's word carried much weight for Hana's mother. Pressed by the two men, she consulted her other daughters and their husbands. She discussed the matter carefully with her brother and asked the village priest. Finally, she agreed to an exchange of family histories and an investigation was begun into Taro Takeda's family, his education, and his health, so they would be assured there was no insanity or tuberculosis or police records concealed in his family's past. Soon Hana's uncle was devoting his energies entirely to serving as go-between for Hana's mother and Taro Takeda's father.

A. List twelve words from the passage that have two syllables. (Do not list proper nouns—words that begin with capital letters.) Say each word aloud to decide how many syllables it has. Draw a line between the syllables of each word.

_______________ _______________ _______________

_______________ _______________ _______________

_______________ _______________ _______________

_______________ _______________ _______________

B. With a partner, go through one or two of the selections in your literature book to find at least two more examples of words following each of the rules on the previous page. Then, think of words you both use in your everyday speech, and come up with at least one more example for each of the rules. Finally, look through your list and circle any syllables that can stand by themselves as words. Look up the meaning of each of these syllables. Then, explain how the syllable contributes to the overall meaning of the word.

RECOGNIZING WORD ROOTS

Introduction

In the English language, many words have a "core" section, or root. Consider, for example, the word *prediction*. *Pre* and *tion* attach to the root, *dic*, which means "say" in Latin. A prediction is something "said before" an event happens.

Some common roots include *grim* in *grimness*, *happy* in *unhappiness*, and *warn* in *forewarned*. You might say that roots are the building blocks of our language. Roots are an important reading and vocabulary tool, because they can help you figure out the meaning of words that are unfamiliar.

Read the passage below from "An Episode of War" by Stephen Crane. Look for other root words.

> The low white tents of the hospital were grouped around an old schoolhouse. There was here a singular commotion. In the foreground two ambulances interlocked wheels in the deep mud. The drivers were tossing the blame of it back and forth, gesticulating and berating, while from the ambulances, both crammed with wounded, there came an occasional groan.

There are several roots in the above passage. For example, notice the word *commotion*. When you encounter an unfamiliar word like *commotion* in your reading, see if the word contains a familiar root. In this case, the root of *commotion* is *motion*, which means "movement." When you see that root together with the prefix *com-* (or *con-*), which means "together, with," you can infer that the word *commotion* means "confusion, bustle, noisy rushing about." On the chart below, you will see how three words from the passage—*commotion, foreground,* and *interlocked*—are formed from root words. Notice that *foreground* is formed from the root *ground* and the prefix *fore-*, meaning "before," and that *interlocked* is formed from the root *lock* and the prefix *inter-*, meaning "between."

Word	Root	Meaning of Root	Meaning of Word
commotion	motion	movement	confusion, bustle
foreground	ground	place, area	part of a scene that is nearest the viewer
interlocked	locked	join, fasten	joined with one another

Practice

Below, you'll find a passage from "An Episode of War" by Stephen Crane. As you read the passage, look for words that have been formed from the roots listed in the chart below. Write these larger words in the first column of the chart. Then, write the meaning of the root, and think about how knowing the root's meaning can help you understand the meaning of the larger word. Write the meaning of the word in the last column of the chart.

As the wounded officer passed from the line of battle, he was enabled to see many things which as a participant in the fight were unknown to him. He saw a general on a black horse gazing over the lines of blue infantry in the green woods which veiled his problems. An aide galloped furiously, dragged his horse suddenly to a halt, saluted, and presented a paper. It was, for a wonder, precisely like a historical painting.

To the rear of the general and his staff a group, composed of a bugler, two or three orderlies, and the bearer of the corps standard,[5] all upon maniacal horses, were working like slaves to hold their ground, preserve their respectful interval, while the shells boomed in the air about them, and caused their chargers to make furious quivering leaps.

5. **corps standard (kôr):** Flag or banner representing a military unit.

Word	Root	Meaning of Root	Meaning of Word
1.	able		
2.	part		
3.	know		
4.	fury		
5.	sudden		
6.	precise		
7.	history		
8.	bugle		
9.	order		
10.	respect		

PREFIXES/SUFFIXES

Introduction

A **prefix** is a letter or letters attached to the front of a word or root to create a new word (for example, *dis*continue, *pre*historic, *be*dazzle). A **suffix** is a letter or letters attached to the end of a word or root to create a new word (for example, respect*ful*, read*able*).

By adding prefixes and suffixes to existing words, you can vastly expand your vocabulary. Learning the meaning of prefixes and suffixes will also help you to piece together the meanings of some unfamiliar words.

While you are reading, you can often figure out a word you don't know by breaking it down into its parts. For example, suppose you come across the word *unpleasantness* in your reading. You can decode the word by breaking it down into three parts (*un-pleasant-ness*):

1. *un-*, a prefix meaning "not" or "the opposite of"
2. *pleasant*, a word meaning "agreeable to the mind or senses"
3. *-ness*, a suffix meaning "a state, quality, or condition"

When you look at the word parts, you realize that *unpleasantness* means "the state of not being agreeable to the mind or senses."

The chart below lists several common prefixes and suffixes and explains what they mean. Study the chart so that you can recall these meanings when you are reading a textbook or story. Knowledge of prefixes and suffixes will save you a lot of time when you are trying to decode words as you read.

Prefix	Meaning	Suffix	Meaning
be-	completely, excessively	*-er*	one that performs a certain task
circum-	around, about	*-est*	the most, forms the superlative degree
dis-	not	*-graph*	something written or drawn
in-	not; in, into within	*-ly*	in the manner of
pre-	before, prior to	*-ment*	action, process
un-	opposite of	*-ness*	state, quality, degree
re-	again, anew	*-ology*	science, study
non-	the opposite of	*-ty*	condition, quality

Practice

As you read the passage below from "A Retrieved Reformation" by O. Henry, suppose that you don't know the meanings of the words *disregarding, leisurely, unlocking,* and *finest.* These words are listed on the chart below the passage. On the chart, write any prefix or suffix contained in these words and what the prefix or suffix means. Then, figure out the meaning of each word, and write that meaning in the last column of the chart.

Disregarding the song of the birds, the waving green trees, and the smell of the flowers, Jimmy headed straight for a restaurant. There he tasted the first sweet joys of liberty in the shape of a chicken dinner. From there he proceeded leisurely to the depot and boarded his train. Three hours set him down in a little town near the state line. He went to the café of one Mike Dolan and shook hands with Mike, who was alone behind the bar. . . .

He got his key and went upstairs, unlocking the door of a room at the rear. Everything was just as he had left it. There on the floor was still Ben Price's collar-button that had been torn from that eminent detective's shirt-band when they had overpowered Jimmy to arrest him. Pulling out from the wall a folding-bed, Jimmy slid back a panel in the wall and dragged out a dust-covered suitcase. He opened this and gazed fondly at the finest set of burglar's tools in the East.

Word	Prefix	Suffix	Word Meaning
1. disregarding			
2. leisurely			
3. unlocking			
4. finest			

Vocabulary
STRATEGY

INFLECTED FORMS: PLURALS AND TENSES

Introduction

An **inflection** is a sound that is added to the end of a word. It changes the word's meaning in some way. Compare the two words *tax* and *taxes*. The sound /iz/ has been added to the stem word *tax* and changes its meaning from singular to plural. "Taxes" is what is called an *inflected form*. The *-es* is the inflection, a special kind of suffix. In English, the sound of the inflections *-s, -es,* or *-ies* is used to change many singular nouns to plural nouns.

Inflections are also used to change the tense of verbs. For example, *register* and *registered*. Notice how the addition of the sound /ed/ changes this verb from the present to the past tense.

There are other uses of inflections in English but these are two of the most important. Understanding how inflections are used will increase your understanding of grammar and help you be a better writer.

Read the passage below from *Travels with Charley* by John Steinbeck. Notice that the verbs *traveled, stopped, gathered, listened, looked,* and *impaired* are all inflected forms.

> Once I traveled about in an old bakery wagon, double-doored rattler with a mattress on its floor. I stopped where people stopped or gathered, I listened and looked and felt, and in the process had a picture of my country the accuracy of which was impaired only by my own shortcomings.

The stems of the inflected verbs are: *travel, stop, gather, listen, look,* and *impair.* The inflected forms let you know that all of the action takes place in the past. The narrator is telling the reader what happened. Inflections are also important in subject-verb agreement. For example, in the present tense you would say "Steinbeck travels," not "Steinbeck traveled." Notice that the *-s* inflection is used here. This is the same sound used to change some singular nouns to plurals.

Practice

Below is another passage from *Travels with Charley* by John Steinbeck. Read the passage carefully, and watch for both plural and tense inflections. (*Hint:* Watch for plural nouns and for verbs in the past tense.)

> A little farther along I stopped at a small house, a section of war-surplus barracks, it looked, but painted white with yellow trim, and with the dying vestiges of a garden, frosted-down geraniums and a few clusters of chrysanthemums, little button things yellow and red-brown. I walked up the path with the certainty that I was being regarded from behind the white window curtains. An old woman answered my knock and gave me the drink of water I asked for and nearly talked my arm off. She was hungry to talk, frantic to talk, about her relatives, her friends, and how she wasn't used to this.

A. List two inflected nouns from the passage above. How does the inflection change their meaning?

____

____

B. List five inflected verbs from the passage above. List those with /ed/ sound endings in one list and those with /t/ sound endings in another. How do the inflections change the meaning of the verbs?

____

____

NAME _______________________________________ **DATE** ___________

CONTEXT CLUES

Introduction

When you read an unfamiliar word, you can use **context clues** to figure out its meaning. Context clues are clues in the text surrounding a word. Look for context clues in the sentence that contains the unfamiliar word or in the phrases or sentences nearby.

Model 1

The following passage is from "Lights in the Night" by Annie Dillard. In the underlined part of the sentence, Dillard describes her baby sister Amy when Amy is asleep. Notice how this description might help readers define the word *serene*.

> All night long she slept smoothly in a series of pleasant and serene, if artificial-looking, positions, a faint smile on her closed lips, as if she were posing for an ad for sheets.

Unfamiliar Word	Context Clues	Definition
serene	smoothly, pleasant, a faint smile on her closed lips, as if she were posing for an ad for sheets	calm, peaceful

Model 2

Dillard uses the word *luminous* in the following passage. Study the underlined words to find context clues that help define the word. As you read the passage, create a definition for the word *luminous* in your mind. Then compare your definition with the one in the chart below.

> I lay alone and was almost asleep when the thing entered the room by flattening itself against the open door and sliding in. It was a transparent, **luminous** oblong. I could see the door whiten at its touch; I could see the blue wall turn pale where it raced over it, and see the maple headboard of Amy's bed glow.

Unfamiliar Word	Context Clues	Definition
luminous	transparent, whiten, pale, glow	shining, bright

Practice

Part I

Below is another passage from "Lights in the Night" by Annie Dillard.
Read the passage and then complete the chart.

> Figuring it out was as memorable as the oblong itself. Figuring it out was a long and forced ascent to the very rim of being, to the membrane of skin that both separates and connects the inner life and the outer world. I climbed deliberately from the depths like a diver who releases the monster in his arms and hauls himself hand over hand up an anchor chain till he meets the ocean's sparkling membrane and bursts through it; he sights the sunlit, becalmed hull of his boat, which had bulked so ominously from below.

Unfamiliar Word	Context Clues	Definition
ascent		
membrane		
ominously		

Part II

The following passage is from "Why Leaves Turn Color in the Fall" by Diane Ackerman. As you read the passage, circle the context clues that might help you define the underlined words. Then, complete the chart on the next page.

> The stealth of autumn catches one unaware. Was that a goldfinch perching in the early September woods, or just the first turning leaf? A red-winged blackbird or a sugar maple closing up shop for the winter? Keen-eyed as leopards, we stand still and squint hard, looking for signs of movement. Early-morning frost sits heavily on the grass, and turns barbed wire into a string of stars. On a distant hill, a small square of yellow appears to be a lighted stage. At last the truth dawns on us: Fall is staggering in, right on schedule, with its baggage of chilly nights, macabre holidays, and spectacular, heart-stoppingly beautiful leaves. Soon the leaves will start cringing on the trees, and roll up in clenched fists before they actually fall off. Dry seedpods will rattle like tiny gourds. But first there will be weeks of gushing color so bright, so pastel, so confettilike, that people will travel up and down the East Coast just to stare at it—a whole season of leaves.

NAME _______________________________________ **DATE** _____________

Part II (continued)

Unfamiliar Word	Context Clues	Definition
stealth		
squint		
spectacular		
cringing		

ACTIVE READING: SET A PURPOSE

Introduction

Different types of writing present different reasons for reading. For example, we read textbooks for a different reason than we might read magazines. When reading a textbook you might skim for information to prepare for a test. When reading a magazine, you might read quickly for entertainment. Before sitting down to read, you might want to set a purpose for reading.

Setting a purpose for reading involves identifying specific questions that you will answer during reading. By asking yourself specific questions before you begin, you direct your attention to the key ideas in the passage. You can get an idea of what the selection is about by looking at the:

- title
- subheadings
- illustrations

You might also want to read the first sentence or passage for further information. Use three steps to help you set a purpose:

1. Study the title and illustrations.

2. Read the first sentence or paragraph.

3. Look for clues in the text (is the writing informative or entertainment?)

Model

Read the following beginning of a passage from "The United States *vs.* Susan B. Anthony" by Margaret Truman. Think of your own questions that you could use to set a purpose for reading this selection. Then compare your questions to the ones below.

> Susan B. Anthony was a stern and single-minded woman. Like most crusaders for causes—especially unpopular causes—she had little time for fun and games. But I have a sneaky feeling that behind her severe manner and unremitting devotion to duty, she may actually have had a sense of humor. Let me tell you about my favorite episode in Susan B. Anthony's career, and perhaps you'll agree.

Questions

Why would you read this passage? What information might you expect to find?

Purpose for Reading

- To find out more about Susan B. Anthony's crusade for an unpopular cause
- To find out more about her sense of humor

Practice

A. Below is another passage from "The United States *vs*. Susan B. Anthony" by Margaret Truman. Read the passage, and then answer the questions below.

The following Tuesday, November 5, was Election Day. Most of the poll inspectors in Rochester had read the editorial in the *Union and Advertiser* and were too intimidated to allow any of the women who had registered to vote. Only in the Eighth Ward did the males weaken. Maybe the inspectors were *Democrat and Chronicle* readers, or perhaps they were more afraid of Susan B. Anthony than they were of the law. Whatever the reason, when Susan and her sisters showed up at the polls shortly after 7A.M., there was only a minimum of fuss. A couple of inspectors were hesitant about letting the women vote, but when Susan assured them that she would pay all their legal expenses if they were prosecuted, the men relented, and one by one, the women took their ballots and stepped into the voting booth. There were no insults or sneers, no rude remarks. They marked their ballots, dropped them into the ballot box, and returned to their homes.

Answer the following questions.

1. What do you think might be the purpose or purposes for reading the passage? Why?

   ____

   ____

2. List at least six details you learned about Election Day from reading this passage.

   a. ____________________   d. ____________________

   b. ____________________   e. ____________________

   c. ____________________   f. ____________________

B. Challenge!
   List three different kinds of books or written texts you might read on your own and your purpose for reading them.

Type of Book or Text	Purpose for Reading
1.	
2.	
3.	

ACTIVE READING: PREDICT

Introduction

When you use what you *know* to explain what you *think* is going to happen, you are making a **prediction**. Predictions are based on two factors:
- information from the story
- knowledge from your own personal experience

Making predictions can make reading more exciting because you become actively involved with what you are reading.

Making Predictions: Three Steps

Step 1

Ask yourself what you know about the story and the characters so far; look for descriptions and clues in the text and make notes to yourself about those clues and details.

Step 2

Ask yourself what your own personal experiences have taught you about the details you wrote in your notes.

Step 3

Based on what you discovered in steps 1 and 2, ask yourself what you think will happen. Write your predictions down on a piece of paper.

Reading Tip

To help you make predictions in your reading, think about other stories and books you have read.
- What predictions did you make?
- Was the story different from your expectations? If so, how?
- What surprised you about the story if anything?
- Were your predictions correct?

NAME _______________________________   **DATE** _______________

Practice

Suppose that you were about to read a descriptive essay entitled "Forest Fire" by Anaïs Nin. Answer the following question.

1. What would the title "Forest Fire" lead you to expect about the incidents in the essay?

   ____

   ____

Read this passage from "Forest Fire." Answer the questions below it.

A man rushed in to announce he had seen smoke on Monrovia Peak. As I looked out of the window I saw the two mountains facing the house on fire. The entire rim burning wildly in the night. The flames, driven by hot Santa Ana winds[2] from the desert, were as tall as the tallest trees, the sky already tinted coral, and the crackling noise of burning trees, the ashes and the smoke were already increasing. The fire raced along, sometimes descending behind the mountain where I could only see the glow, sometimes descending toward us. I thought of the foresters in danger. I made coffee for the weary men who came down occasionally with horses they had led out, or with old people from the isolated cabins. They were covered with soot from their battle with the flames.

2. **Santa Ana winds:** Hot desert winds from the east or northeast in southern California.

2. What do you think will happen in the next few paragraphs of the essay?

   ____

3. What details in the passage helped you make this prediction?

   ____

Now read another passage from "Forest Fire," and answer the questions.

The blaring loudspeakers of passing police cars warned us to prepare to evacuate in case the wind changed and drove the fire in our direction. What did I wish to save? I thought only of the diaries. I appeared on the porch carrying a huge stack of diary volumes, preparing to pack them in the car. A reporter for the Pasadena *Star News* was taking pictures of the evacuation. He came up, very annoyed with me. "Hey, lady, next time could you bring out something more important than all those old papers? Carry some clothes on the next trip. We gotta have human interest in these pictures!"

A week later, the danger was over.

4. How were your predictions about what would happen like the actual events in the essay?

   ____

5. How were your predictions different from the events in the essay?

   ____

ACTIVE READING: QUESTION AND CLARIFY

Introduction

Question: Asking yourself questions as you read can help improve your reading comprehension. The first step is to identify what is confusing to you.

Clarify: Often, the answer to your question can be found right in the text, either at an earlier point or later in the text. When you have a question while reading:

- Stop to think.
- Look back over the material you have already read to try to find clues to the answer.
- Continue reading, keeping your question in mind. Often you'll discover the answer later in the text.

Model

Read the passage below from "Achieving the American Dream" by Mario Cuomo, and note the interrupter questions in italics.

In the Provincia di Salerno[1] just outside the Italian city of Naples, a laborer named Andrea Cuomo asked Immaculata Giordano to marry him.

This couple has the same last name as the author. I wonder if they are his parents?

The young woman accepted under one condition: that the couple immigrate to the far-off land of her dreams—America.

What does "immigrate" mean?

Andrea Cuomo agreed, and after marrying, the Cuomos made the long voyage to New York Harbor in the late 1920s. The young couple left the life, the language, the land, the family, and the friends they knew, arriving in Lady Liberty's shadow with no money, unable to speak English, and without any education. They were filled with both hope and apprehension.

I see—"immigrate" means to go to leave your own country and settle down in a new country.

All that my parents brought to their new home was their burning desire to climb out of poverty on the strength of their labor.

I was right—the author is the couple's son.

They believed that hard work would bring them and their children better lives and help them achieve the American Dream.

1. **Provincia di Salerno:** Region surrounding Salerno, a seaport in southern Italy.

Practice

Below is a passage from "Coyote Steals the Sun and Moon," a Zuñi myth retold by Richard Erdoes and Alfonso Ortiz. As you read the passage, ask yourself questions about what is happening.

> …They went on as before, but now Coyote had the box. Soon Eagle was far ahead, and Coyote lagged behind a hill where Eagle couldn't see him. "I wonder what the light looks like, inside there," he said to himself. "Why shouldn't I take a peek? Probably there's something extra in the box, something good that Eagle wants to keep to himself."
>
> And Coyote opened the lid. Now, not only was the sun inside, but the moon also. Eagle had put them both together, thinking that it would be easier to carry one box than two.
>
> As soon as Coyote opened the lid, the moon escaped, flying high into the sky. At once all the plants shriveled up and turned brown. Just as quickly, all the leaves fell off the trees, and it was winter. Trying to catch the moon and put it back into the box, Coyote ran in pursuit as it skipped away from him. Meanwhile the sun flew out and rose into the sky. It drifted far away, and the peaches, squashes, and melons shriveled up with cold.
>
> Eagle turned and flew back to see what had delayed Coyote. "You fool! Look what you've done!" he said. "You let the sun and moon escape, and now it's cold." Indeed, it began to snow, and Coyote shivered. "Now your teeth are chattering," Eagle said, "and it's your fault that cold has come into the world."
>
> It's true. If it weren't for Coyote's curiosity and mischief making, we wouldn't have winter; we could enjoy summer all the time.

1. While you were reading the passage, what questions did you have?

____

____

____

____

2. What information in the passage helped clarify the answers to these questions?

____

____

____

____

ACTIVE READING: CONNECT

Introduction

There are many ways to respond to something that you are reading. One of the most natural responses is to think how the literature relates to your own experiences or to another text that you have read. As you read, you may **connect** to a character or to something that character says or does. Sometimes, you will be reminded of another story you once read or something that you recently learned. Making connections as you read is important because it allows you to relate to the text in your own personal way.

To make connections in your reading, ask yourself questions such as those below. They will help you to become a more active reader by giving you ideas about how you can connect to what you are reading.

Questions to Help You Connect

- What do I relate to about this character?
- Am I like this person? Do I know someone like this person?
- Would I have done or said the same thing as this person?
- Is there anything in this story that is similar to my life, my own experiences, or the experiences of someone that I know?
- In what ways is this story like another story that I have read?

Model

The passage below, from "The Medicine Bag" by Virginia Driving Hawk Sneve, describes some young people's feelings about an elderly relative.

As you read the passage, connect it to your own experiences, ideas, or perhaps another story you have read. The connections you make may be similar to or different from some of the sample connections shown below.

> We never showed our friends Grandpa's picture. Not that we were ashamed of him, but because we knew that the glamorous tales we told didn't go with the real thing. Our friends would have laughed at the picture because Grandpa wasn't tall and stately like TV Indians. His hair wasn't in braids but hung in stringy, gray strands on his neck, and he was old. He was our great-grandfather, and he didn't live in a tepee,[3] but all by himself in a part log, part tarpaper shack on the Rosebud Reservation[4] in South Dakota. So when Grandpa came to visit us, I was so ashamed and embarrassed I could've died.

3. **tepee:** Cone-shaped tent of animal skins; used by the Plains Indians.
4. **Rosebud Reservation:** Small Indian reservation in south central South Dakota.

Possible Connections

- I know someone who tells interesting stories about her grandfather.
- I've seen quite a few films and TV movies with Indians in them.
- My older sister sometimes seems embarrassed by Grandma's slightly foreign accent.
- I read an article about Indian reservations the other day in a newsmagazine.

NAME _______________________________   **DATE** _____________

Practice

Below is another passage from "The Medicine Bag" by Virginia Driving
Hawk Sneve. As you read the selection, think about how you connect to
it and respond by writing your ideas in the appropriate sections below.

> "You guys want some lemonade or something?" I offered. No one
> answered. They were listening to Grandpa as he started telling how he'd
> killed the deer from which his vest was made.
>
> Grandpa did most of the talking while my friends were there. I was so
> proud of him and amazed at how respectfully quiet my buddies were. Mom
> had to chase them home at supper time. As they left, they shook Grandpa's
> hand again and said to me,
>
> "Martin, he's really great!"
>
> "Yeah, man! Don't blame you for keeping him to yourself."
>
> "Can we come back?"
>
> But after they left, Mom said, "No more visitors for a while, Martin.
> Grandpa won't admit it, but his strength hasn't returned. He likes having
> company, but it tires him."

1. Do you know anyone that any of these characters calls to mind?

____

____

2. Do any of the events in this passage remind you of experiences in
   your own life? Explain.

____

____

____

3. Do you connect with any of the feelings that the different characters
   have? Tell about times that come to your mind when you felt the
   same way.

____

____

____

4. Does this passage remind you of another story? In what way?

____

____

____

ACTIVE READING: SQ3R

Introduction

Most of the time, people read either for pleasure or to learn about new things. When "reading to learn" it is helpful to use the **SQ3R** strategy. This strategy helps you understand and remember what you read, especially when you are reading a difficult or unfamiliar text.

SQ3R stands for the five steps a reader can use to remember information.

Survey	Survey the text and get a general idea of what it is about. Try reading the first sentence of each paragraph.
Question	Keep in mind questions you have as you look over the selection. What do you want to find out about in the selection? What looks unclear to you?
Read	Read the text carefully from the beginning. Pause to think about what you are reading and to make sure you understand it. Look up unknown words and reread difficult sentences or paragraphs.
Recite	See how well you understood and remember the text by reciting what you learned out loud. Recite the information to yourself or to a friend. **Helpful Hint:** Try to answer these questions: Who? What? Where? When? Why? How?
Review	Summarize the text and think about the main ideas by talking with someone else about it. You may also want to make an outline, use note cards, or make an illustration to help you remember key points.

Practice

Practice using the SQ3R strategy with the passage below from "Eleanor Roosevelt" by William J. Jacobs. Do not read the entire passage first. Follow the steps below.

I. Survey

What does this passage seem like it will be about?

____

II. Question

Write some questions that you have.

____

____

III. Read

Read the passage. Pause as you read to make sure that you understand it.

> Eleanor was born in a fine townhouse in Manhattan. Her family also owned an elegant mansion along the Hudson River, where they spent weekends and summers. As a child Eleanor went to fashionable parties. A servant took care of her and taught her to speak French. Her mother, the beautiful Anna Hall Roosevelt, wore magnificent jewels and fine clothing. Her father, Elliott Roosevelt, had his own hunting lodge and liked to sail and to play tennis and polo. Elliott, who loved Eleanor dearly, was the younger brother of Theodore Roosevelt, who in 1901 became president of the United States. The Roosevelt family, one of America's oldest, wealthiest families, was respected and admired.
>
> To the outside world it might have seemed that Eleanor had everything that any child could want—everything that could make her happy. But she was not happy. Instead her childhood was very sad.
>
> Almost from the day of her birth, October 11, 1884, people noticed that she was an unattractive child. As she grew older, she could not help but notice her mother's extraordinary beauty, as well as the beauty of her aunts and cousins. Eleanor was plain looking, ordinary, even, as some called her, homely. For a time she had to wear a bulky brace on her back to straighten her crooked spine.

IV. Recite

Verbalize what you have just read by telling yourself or a friend about it.

V. Review

In your notebook, write a brief summary or outline of the passage.

ACTIVE READING: IDENTIFY MAIN IDEAS AND SUPPORTING DETAILS

Introduction

The **main idea** of a passage is its central and most important idea. Effective readers look for this central idea as they read. The main idea can appear at the beginning, middle, or end of a passage. Writers reinforce their main ideas with **supporting details**. These words, phrases, or sentences tell something about the main idea. They can be facts, statistics, dates, names, opinions, or details. The main idea of a passage can be stated clearly in one sentence in the selection. This is called a **stated main idea**. Sometimes the main idea is not stated in any one sentence but is a summary of the information in the passage. This is called an **implied main idea**. When you are reading, begin to identify the main idea, whether stated or implied, and look for its supporting details.

Model 1

In the following passage from "Hokusai: The Old Man Mad About Drawing," by Stephen Longstreet, the underlined sentence is the stated main idea. Each sentence that follows provides support for the idea.

> Hokusai never stayed long with a period or style, but was always off and running to something new. A great show-off, he painted with his fingers, toothpicks, a bottle, an eggshell; he worked left- handed, from the bottom up, and from left to right. Once he painted two sparrows on a grain of rice.

Model 2

In this example from "Saving the Wetlands" by Barbara A. Lewis, the main idea is implied rather than stated directly.

> Andy remembers sitting on the glacial rocks by the stream in the middle of winter, eating baloney sandwiches. In the warmer months, he and Nicholas and Elizabeth played tag in the stream, jumping on the slippery rocks, soaking their shoes, socks, and jeans. When fall came, they gathered brilliant red leaves from swamp maples and golden oak, while their mother picked dried grape vines for wreaths....

The implied main idea might be stated as follows:
The stream was a delightful place at every season of the year.

NAME _______________________________________   DATE _____________

Practice

Part I

Below is a passage from "Brown *vs.* Board of Education" by Walter Dean Myers. Read the passage and answer the questions that follow.

> From the end of the Civil War in 1865 to the early 1950's, many public schools in both the North and South were segregated. Segregation was different in the different sections of the country. In the North most of the schools were segregated *de facto;*[1] that is, the law allowed blacks and whites to go to school together, but they did not actually always attend the same schools. Since a school is generally attended by children living in its neighborhood, wherever there were predominantly African-American neighborhoods there were, "in fact," segregated schools. In many parts of the country, however, and especially in the South, the segregation was *de jure,*[2] meaning that there were laws which forbade blacks to attend the same schools as whites.

1. *de facto* (defak' to): Latin for "existing in actual fact."
2. *de jure* (dejur' e): Latin for "by right or legal establishment."

1. What statement best expresses the main idea of this passage?

   ____

   ____

   ____

   ____

2. Is the main idea implied or stated? ___________________________

3. Identify four supporting details in this passage. Write the details in the spaces provided.

   a. ___________________________   c. ___________________________

   ___________________________   ___________________________

   ___________________________   ___________________________

   b. ___________________________   d. ___________________________

   ___________________________   ___________________________

   ___________________________   ___________________________

NAME ____   DATE _____________

Part II

Below is a passage from "Shooting Stars" by Hal Borland. Read the
passage and answer the questions that follow.

> Most people watching meteors will be satisfied if they see ten or twenty
> in an hour of watching. On special occasions, however, the meteors seem
> to come in droves. The most remarkable meteor shower I ever heard of
> was seen by a distinguished astronomer, Professor Denison Olmstead, in
> New Haven, Connecticut, on the night of November 12, 1833. He was
> watching the Leonids, which seem to come from directly overhead and
> race downward toward the horizon in all directions. He reported that
> meteors fell "like flakes of snow." He estimated that he saw 240,000
> meteors in nine hours that night. He said they ranged in size from mere
> streaks of light to "globes of the moon's diameter." If he had not been a
> notable astronomer whose accuracy was beyond question, such state-
> ments would seem ridiculous. But there is no reason to doubt what he
> reported. He had seen one of the most unusual meteor showers ever
> reported. What he watched should be called a meteor storm rather than
> a shower.

1. What statement best expresses the main idea of this passage?

   ____

   ____

   ____

   ____

2. Is the main idea implied or stated? _______________________________

3. Identify four supporting details in this passage. Write the details in
   the spaces provided.

   a. ____________________   c. ____________________

      ____________________   ____________________

      ____________________   ____________________

   b. ____________________   d. ____________________

      ____________________   ____________________

      ____________________   ____________________

Part III

Below is a passage from "How to Be Polite Online" by Virginia Shea. Read the passage and answer the questions that follow.

> The fact that most network interactions are limited to written words can be the source of misunderstandings. Fortunately, clever network users have had years to deal with this. They've created a shorthand to help communicate the tone that you'd otherwise get from the other person's voice, facial expressions, and gestures. These shorthand expressions are known as smileys or emoticons. They're easy to figure out once you get the hang of it. Just remember that they're all sideways faces.
>
> …There are whole books about smileys for those who are interested, including the enjoyable *Smiley Dictionary* by Seth Godin.
>
> People also use abbreviations to express emotional states or to qualify what they're saying….

1. What statement best expresses the main idea of this passage?

   ____

   ____

   ____

   ____

2. Is the main idea implied or stated? _______________________________

3. Identify four supporting details in this passage. Write the details in the spaces provided.

   a. ___________________________   c. ___________________________

   ___________________________   ___________________________

   ___________________________   ___________________________

   b. ___________________________   d. ___________________________

   ___________________________   ___________________________

   ___________________________   ___________________________

NAME _______________________________   DATE __________

MAKE INFERENCES

Introduction

Writers don't always describe everything that is happening. It is up to the reader to figure out why characters may be acting or feeling a certain way. When readers draw these types of conclusions they are **making inferences**. Often, making inferences requires readers to "read between the lines." Your own experiences and prior knowledge about people, places, ideas, and events will help you to make inferences or reasonable guesses as you read. In addition, use whatever textual clues there are in order to draw certain conclusions. These inferences will help you to understand the selection better and to identify what the author is trying to communicate.

Keep this equation in mind to understand how to make inferences.

Textual Clues　+　What You Know　=　Inference

Model

Read the passage below from "Up the Slide" by Jack London. Then look at the chart to see how certain inferences were made.

> When Clay Dillam left the tent to get a sled-load of firewood, he expected to be back in half an hour. So he told Swanson, who was cooking the dinner. Swanson and he belonged to different outfits, located about twenty miles apart on the Stewart River, but they had become traveling partners on a trip down the Yukon to Dawson[1] to get the mail.
>
> Swanson had laughed when Clay said he would be back in half an hour. It stood to reason, Swanson said, that good, dry firewood could not be found so close to Dawson; that whatever firewood there was originally had long since been gathered in; that firewood would not be selling at forty dollars a cord if any man could go out and get a sled-load and be back in the time Clay expected to make it.

1. **Yukon...Dawson:** The Yukon River is in the Yukon Territory of northwestern Canada, and Dawson is a town nearby.

Textual Clues	+	What You Know	=	Inference
Clay and Swanson need firewood		Story takes place in a very cold setting		Firewood may be hard to get
Clay and Swanson are from different outfits		People need time to get to know each other		The characters do not know each other very well
Swanson laughs when Clay says he will be back in half an hour		Swanson seems to have good reasons		Clay may be quite inexperienced

Practice

Below is a passage from "Thank You, M'am" by Langston Hughes. As you read the passage, look for clues that help you make inferences about what is happening. Then answer the questions that follow.

> The woman said, "You ought to be my son. I would teach you right from wrong. Least I can do right now is to wash your face. Are you hungry?"
>
> "No'm," said the being-dragged boy. "I just want you to turn me loose."
>
> "Was I bothering *you* when I turned that corner?" asked the woman.
>
> "No'm."
>
> "But you put yourself in contact with *me*," said the woman. "If you think that that contact is not going to last awhile, you got another thought coming. When I get through with you, sir, you are going to remember Mrs. Luella Bates Washington Jones."
>
> Sweat popped out on the boy's face and he began to struggle. Mrs. Jones stopped, jerked him around in front of her, put a half nelson[1] about his neck, and continued to drag him up the street. When she got to her door, she dragged the boy inside, down a hall, and into a large kitchenette-furnished room at the rear of the house. She switched on the light and left the door open.

___

1. **half nelson:** Wrestling hold using one arm.

1. What inference can you make about how the two characters are feeling in this scene?

   ____

   ____

   What clues helped you make this inference?

   ____

   ____

2. What inference can you make about Mrs. Jones's standards and values?

   ____

   What clues helped you make this inference?

   ____

   ____

3. What inference can you make about the place where the events in the story happen?

   ____

   What clues helped you make this inference?

   ____

   ____

CLASSIFY/CATEGORIZE

Introduction

When you **classify** or **categorize**, you arrange things into classes or groups according to a system, For example, dogs and cats are both classified as animals, but each can be further classified into different types of dogs or cats.

This chart may help clarify the relationship of the things to be classified and their division into groups.

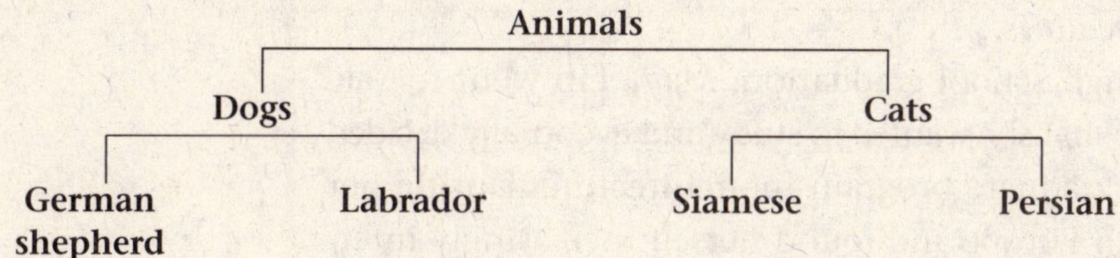

In much of your reading, you will come upon examples of classification. Classifying is a technique that writers use to organize a passage. Writers help readers understand a point they are making by classifying ideas or things into a group. While you are reading, look for examples of this technique. Notice how classifying helps you recognize similarities and differences in a subject and helps explain an idea by providing specific examples or details.

Model

Read the following passage from "Always to Remember: The Vision of Maya Ying Lin," by Brent Ashabranner.

> Announcement of the competition in October, 1980, brought an astonishing response. The Vietnam Veterans Memorial Fund received over five thousand inquiries. They came from every state in the nation and from every field of design; as expected, architects and sculptors were particularly interested. Everyone who inquired received a booklet explaining the criteria. Among the most important: The memorial could not make a political statement about the war; it must contain the names of all persons killed or missing in action in the war; it must be in harmony with its location on the Mall.

Above, Brent Ashabranner classifies/categorizes the inquiries about the competition and the criteria for the design of the Vietnam Veterans Memorial.

Inquiries About the Competition	Criteria for the Design of the Vietnam Veterans Memorial
• from every state in the nation • from every field of design • especially from architects and sculptors	• criteria listed in booklet • most important criteria included no political statement, names of all persons killed or missing in action, harmony with location

NAME _______________________________   **DATE** _________

Practice

Below is another passage from "Always to Remember: The Vision of
Maya Ying Lin" by Brent Ashabranner. Read the passage and follow the
instructions below.

> Maya Lin grew up in an environment of art and literature. She was inter-
> ested in sculpture and made both small and large sculptural figures, one
> cast in bronze. She learned silversmithing and made jewelry. She was
> surrounded by books and read a great deal, especially fantasies such as
> *The Hobbit* and *Lord of the Rings*....[1]
>
> A covaledictorian at high school graduation, Maya Lin went to Yale
> without a clear notion of what she wanted to study and eventually decided
> to major in Yale's undergraduate program in architecture. During her
> junior year she studied in Europe and found herself increasingly inter-
> ested in cemetery architecture. "In Europe there's very little space, so
> graveyards are used as parks," she said. "Cemeteries are cities of the dead
> in European countries, but they are also living gardens. "

1. *The Hobbit* and *Lord of the Rings:* Mythical novels by the English author and scholar
J. R. R. Tolkien (1892-1973).

1. What kinds of activities is Ashabranner classifying in the first
   paragraph of this passage? In the second paragraph?

   ____

   ____

   ____

   ____

2. How does the classifying of these activities aid your understanding of
   Maya Lin's interests and personality?

   ____

   ____

   ____

   ____

3. **Challenge!**
   Choose an interest of yours that is a high priority in your life. It might be
   a hobby, a sport, reading, listening to music or performing it, watching
   television, or spending time with your friends. Write a paragraph that clas-
   sifies your activities to show how important this special interest is to you.

   ____

   ____

   ____

   ____

COMPARE AND CONTRAST

Introduction

As you read, look for the writer's use of comparisons and contrasts. A writer uses **comparison** to show how things are similar and uses **contrast** to show how things are different. While reading, look for clue words that may help you recognize a comparison or contrast. Clue words and phrases that may signal a comparison are *like, similar to,* and *in the same way.* Words and phrases that may signal a contrast are *but, different from,* and *however.*

Model

Read the passage below from "Amigo Brothers" by Piri Thomas. Look for the comparisons and contrasts and compare them to the ones below.

> Antonio was fair, lean, and lanky, while Felix was dark, short, and husky. Antonio's hair was always falling over his eyes, while Felix wore his black hair in a natural Afro style.
>
> Each youngster had a dream of someday becoming lightweight champion of the world. Every chance they had the boys worked out, sometimes at the Boy's Club on 10th Street and Avenue A and sometimes at the pro's gym on 14th Street.

Comparison

- Both boys have a dream of becoming lightweight champion.
- Both boys work out every chance they have.

These statements show the similarities between the two boys.

Contrast

- Antonio is fair and lean, while Felix is dark and husky.
- Antonio's hair falls over his eyes, but Felix wears his hair in a natural Afro style.

These statements show the differences between the two boys.

NAME _______________________________________ **DATE** _____________

Practice

Below is a passage from "Harriet Tubman: Guide to Freedom" by Ann Petry. Read the passage and answer the questions below.

> Harriet had found it hard to leave the warmth and friendliness, too. But she urged them on. For a while, as they walked, they seemed to carry in them a measure of contentment; some of the serenity and cleanliness of that big warm kitchen lived on inside them. But as they walked farther and farther away from the warmth and from the light, the cold and the darkness entered into them. They fell silent, sullen, suspicious. She waited for the moment when some one of them would turn mutinous.

1. As they walk farther and farther, how does the group's mood contrast with the feelings they had in the big warm kitchen?

   ____

   ____

2. Circle the words that help you recognize comparisons and contrasts.
   a. The warm kitchen was like an island of contentment.
   b. The German farmer spoke slowly, but he was kind and welcoming.
   c. It was hard for the group of fugitive slaves to exchange the security of the farmhouse for the dangers of the cold outdoors.
   d. Harriet Tubman could sense that the group's mood was becoming different from their feelings when they left Maryland.
   e. The fugitives now seemed similar to sailors who might mutiny against their captain.

3. **Challenge!**
   Research living conditions in another country of your choice. List five comparisons and five contrasts to living in your country.

	Compare	Contrast
1.		
2.		
3.		
4.		
5.		

FOLLOW A SEQUENCE OF EVENTS

Introduction

The **sequence of events** in a passage is the chronological, or time, order of those events.

While you read, in order to help you follow the sequence of events, you may want to make a timeline. A timeline not only enables you to follow the series of events but also to see the pattern of events that is developing. To make a timeline, draw a horizontal line. Draw a short vertical line for each important event in the sequence. At each vertical line, write a few words describing the event.

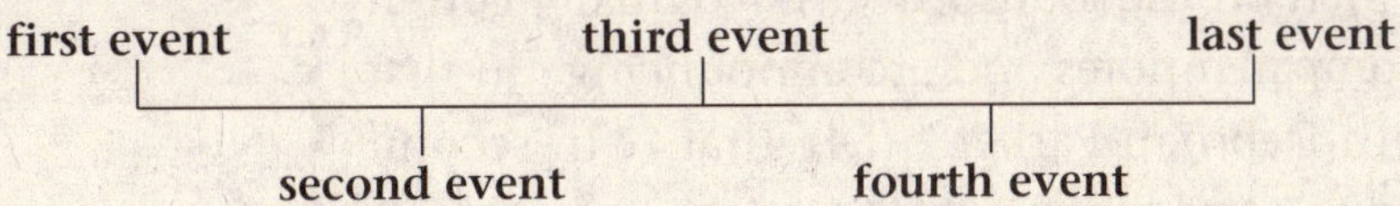

Helpful Hint: Look for clue words that may signal a sequence, such as *first*, *second*, *next*, *then*, *finally*, and *last*.

Model

Make a timeline for the events in this passage from "Harriet Tubman: Guide to Freedom" by Ann Petry. When you have finished your work, compare your timeline to the one below.

> Harriet felt safer now, though there were danger spots ahead. But the biggest part of her job was over. As they went farther and farther north, it grew colder; she was aware of the wind on the Jersey ferry and aware of the cold damp in New York. From New York they went on to Syracuse, where the temperature was even lower....
>
> From Syracuse they went north again, into a colder, snowier city— Rochester. Here they almost certainly stayed with Frederick Douglass....
>
> Late in December 1851, Harriet arrived in St. Catharines, Canada West (now Ontario), with the eleven fugitives. It had taken almost a month to complete this journey; most of the time had been spent getting out of Maryland.

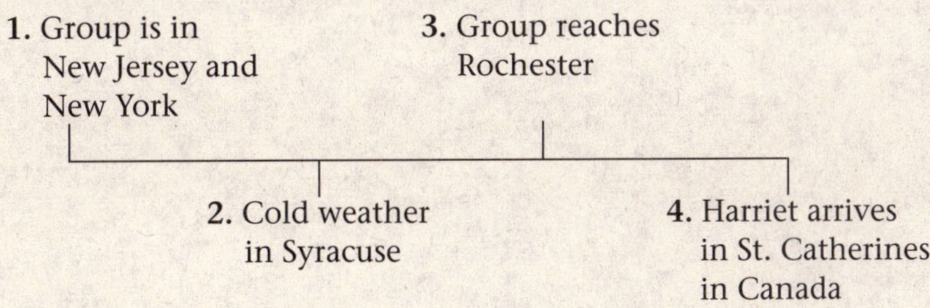

Practice

1. Timeline

Make a timeline for this passage from "Raymond's Run" by Toni Cade Bambara. The horizontal line has already been drawn for you.

So I stand there with my new plans, laughing out loud by this time as Raymond jumps down from the fence and runs over with his teeth showing and his arms down to the side, which no one before him has quite mastered as a running style. And by the time he comes over I'm jumping up and down so glad to see him—my brother Raymond, a great runner in the family tradition. But of course everyone thinks I'm jumping up and down because the men on the loudspeaker have finally gotten themselves together and compared notes and are announcing "In first place—Miss Hazel Elizabeth Deborah Parker." (Dig that.) "In second place—Miss Gretchen P. Lewis." And I look over at Gretchen wondering what the "P" stands for. And I smile.

2. Questions

Use your timeline to answer the following questions.
- What is the first event?
- What two announcements are made on the loudspeaker?
- What does the narrator do at the end of the passage?

NAME _______________________________ **DATE** __________

USE VISUAL AND GRAPHIC CLUES

Introduction

When you read, you can learn all kinds of information. Some information, however, does not come from words. **Visual and graphic aids** are pictorial representations that also help you learn about a subject. Visual and graphic sources of information include the following:

diagrams	lists	maps	charts
illustrations	scale drawings	schedules	tables
timelines	graphs	cartoons	outlines

One kind of visual or graphic aid that you may encounter is a table. A table shows related facts in chart form. Study a portion of a table below from "How to Be Polite Online" by Virginia Shea.

Table 1: Emoticons

:-)	Smile; laugh; "I'm joking"
:-(	Frown; sadness; "Bummer"
;-)	Wink; denotes a pun or sly joke
%-)	Confused but happy
%-(	Confused and unhappy
:-|	Can't decide how to feel; no feelings either way

Which two shorthand expressions are used to express happiness?

____

____

Which two are used to express unhappiness?

____

____

Practice

A. Another kind of graphic aid you will encounter is a schedule. Use the train schedule below to answer the questions that follow.

New York to Washington, D. C.		Washington, D. C. to New York	
Departures	Arrivals	Departures	Arrivals
*6:30 A.M.	9:32 A.M.	*6:00 A.M.	9:14 A.M.
8:40 A.M.	12:30 A.M.	8:15 A.M.	12:20 A.M.
11:15 A.M.	3:05 P.M.	10:45 A.M.	2:40 P.M.
*2:40 P.M.	5:50 P.M.	2:00 P.M.	5:15 P.M.
*5:30 P.M.	8:35 P.M.	*5:45 P.M.	9:00 P.M.

*Express service

1. Which nonstop train leaving New York departs earliest in the morning?

____

2. If you must be in Washington, D.C. by 12 noon, which train must you take from New York?

____

3. When would you arrive in New York if you left Washington, D.C. on the 10:45 A.M. train?

____

4. How long is the trip to New York if you take the 5:45 P.M. train from Washington, D.C.?

____

B. Challenge!
On a separate piece of paper, make a schedule to show when events in your life take place on a typical day.

ADJUST READING RATE

Introduction

Every day you read a variety of different materials, from TV guides to newspaper headlines to the instructions on a test at school. You read some materials more quickly than others. The speed at which you read is called your **reading rate**.

You adjust your reading rate depending on what you are reading and what your purpose is for reading. For example, when you read a story for entertainment, you probably read fairly quickly. On the other hand, when you read a textbook or a magazine article to learn important information, you read more slowly and carefully.

Which of the following—a science fiction tale, a chapter about the history of a foreign country, or a letter from a friend—do you think you would read most quickly? Most slowly? Choosing the appropriate reading rate will help you get the most out of what you read. Before you begin to read, follow these steps to determine which reading rate is right for you:

1. First, consider your purpose for reading.
2. Then, look at the selection to find out how difficult it is to read.
3. Finally, decide whether you should read the selection at a faster, average, or slower rate.

The following guidelines may help you adjust your reading rate to suit your purpose and the type of material you are going to read:

- When you read to learn information or when you read difficult selections that contain unfamiliar words and ideas, read slowly and carefully.
- Read more quickly when you read for entertainment or when you read fairly easy selections about subjects with which you are familiar.

Reading Tips

- Two strategies that will help you read more quickly and efficiently are skimming and scanning. **Skim** a selection to get a general impression about the topic. Do not read every word but look at the selection quickly, noticing the title, headings, words in boldface or italic type, and visual and graphic clues. Skimming a selection before you read will help you determine which reading rate to use.
- **Scan** a selection to find specific information, such as dates and important facts. Read quickly, moving your eyes over the page to locate key words that will help you find the information that you want.
- When you want to learn information and remember details, do a close reading. Read the entire selection slowly word for word.

Practice

Below is a passage from "Columbus" by Joaquin Miller. Before you read, skim the passage to determine which reading rate you will use. Consider why you are reading this passage and how difficult it is for you to read. Then, read the passage, using the reading rate that you selected, and answer the questions below.

Behind him lay the gray Azores,[1]
Behind the Gates of Hercules;[2]
Before him not the ghost of shores;
Before him only shoreless seas.
The good mate said, "Now must we pray,
For lo! the very stars are gone.
Brave Adm'r'l, speak; what shall I say?"
"Why, say: 'Sail on! sail on! and on! '"

"My men grow mutinous day by day;
My men grow ghastly wan and weak."
The stout mate thought of home; a spray
Of salt wave washed his swarthy cheek.
"What shall I say, brave Adm'r'l, say,
If we sight naught[3] but seas at dawn?"
"Why, you shall say at break of day:
'Sail on! sail on! sail on! and on! '"

1. **Azores:** Group of Portuguese islands in the North Atlantic.
2. **Gates of Hercules:** Entrance to the Strait of Gibraltar, between Spain and Africa.
3. **naught:** Nothing.

1. What reading rate—faster, average, or slower—did you select for reading this passage?

2. Why did you choose this reading rate?

3. **Challenge!**
   Find three different types of selections that you are likely to read. (For example, you might consider a magazine article, a recipe, a bus schedule, an instruction manual for a video game, a short story, or another type of selection.) Skim each selection you choose, and decide at what rate you would read it—a faster rate, an average rate, or a slower rate. On a separate sheet of paper, explain why you chose the rate you did for each selection.

ACTIVE READING: ACTIVATE PRIOR KNOWLEDGE

Introduction

What you know before you open a book may decide how you react to it. Using the knowledge you already have about a particular subject can make what you read easier to understand.

In most cases, the subject of an article or story will become clear to you once you have read the first paragraph or two of a piece of writing. At that point, you may want to stop and ask yourself what you already know about the subject.

Reading Tip

Activate prior knowledge by asking yourself the following questions:
1. What is the subject of this piece of writing?
2. What do I already know about this subject?
3. Have I ever read about this subject before? If so, what specific details did I learn about it?

Model

Read the passage below from "Western Wagons" by Stephen Vincent Benét. Identify the subject of the passage. Then, quickly list a few things you know about it on a sheet of paper. Compare your answers to the sample list below.

> They went with axe and rifle, when the trail was still to blaze,
> They went with wife and children, in the prairie-schooner days,
> With banjo and with frying pan—Susanna, don't you cry!
> For I'm off to California to get rich out there or die!
> We've broken land and cleared it, but we're tired of where we are.
> They say that wild Nebraska is a better place by far.
> There's gold in far Wyoming, there's black earth in Ioway,
> So pack up the kids and blankets, for we're moving out today!

Subject: The pioneers are moving West.

1. What I already know:
   - Many pioneers traveled in covered wagons.
   - People hoped to get rich in the California Gold Rush.
   - Pioneers often faced hardships.
2. What I've read about this subject before:
   - I read a book about the pioneers that told how they battled forces of nature like fierce storms, high mountains, and dangerous rivers.

NAME _______________________________   **DATE** _____________

Practice

Below is a passage from "The Other Pioneers" by Roberto Félix Salazar.
Read the passage and then answer the questions that follow it.

Now I must write
Of those of mine who rode these plains
Long years before the Saxon[1] and the Irish came.
Of those who plowed the land and built the towns
And gave the towns soft-woven Spanish names.
Of those who moved across the Rio Grande
Toward the hiss of Texas snake and Indian yell.
Of men who from the earth made thick-walled homes
And from the earth raised churches to their God.
And of the wives who bore them sons
And smiled with knowing joy.

They saw the Texas sun rise golden-red with promised wealth
And saw the Texas sun sink golden yet, with wealth unspent.
"Here," they said. "Here to live and here to love."
"Here is the land for our sons and the sons of our sons."
And they sang the songs of ancient Spain
And they made new songs to fit new needs.

1. **Saxon:** English.

1. Can you think of any towns with Spanish names? If so, list the
   names on the lines below.

   ____

   ____

2. What were the hopes and dreams of the "other pioneers" who came to
   Texas? From your experience, are these goals the same as or different
   from the hopes of pioneers who went West or of the immigrants who
   crossed the Atlantic or Pacific Ocean to reach the United States?

   ____

   ____

3. The poet seems proud of his heritage. Do you know about any
   famous people—musicians, sports stars, actors, or politicians—who
   are proud of their heritage? List one or two of these people below,
   and add a brief comment about why you admire them.

   ____

   ____

KWL

Introduction

KWL is a strategy that you can use to organize your thoughts before and after you read a selection. KWL stands for what you **know**, what you **want to know**, and what you **learn**. A chart like the one below will help you to use the KWL strategy. Simply follow these three steps.

Step 1	Step 2	Step 3
K (What You **Know**)	W (What You **Want to Know**)	L (What You **Learn**)

Model

The passage below is from "A Retrieved Reformation" by O. Henry. By knowing the topic of the selection or by reading the first sentence or two of it, you can complete the first two steps in the KWL strategy. Then, as you read the passage, you can jot down what you learn. Read the passage and then look at the sample KWL chart to see how one reader used the technique to help read the passage.

> A guard came to the prison shoe-shop, where Jimmy Valentine was assid-uously stitching uppers, and escorted him to the front office. There the warden handed Jimmy his pardon, which had been signed that morning by the governor….He had served nearly ten months of a four-year sentence. He had expected to stay only about three months, at the longest. When a man with as many friends on the outside as Jimmy Valentine had is received in the "stir" it is hardly worthwhile to cut his hair.
>
> "Now, Valentine," said the warden, "you'll go out in the morning. Brace up, and make a man of yourself. You're not a bad fellow at heart. Stop cracking safes, and live straight."

K What you **Know**	W What you **Want to Know**	L What you **Learn**
• Prisoners are sometimes released from jail if they are pardoned or paroled.	• I want to know why Jimmy was in jail.	• He was a burglar who cracked safes.
• Most people have a mixture of good and not-so-good traits	• Will Jimmy manage to keep out of trouble?	

NAME _______________________________   **DATE** _____________

Practice

The passage below is from "Tears of Autumn" by Yoshiko Uchida. It is about a young Japanese woman named Hana who has just arrived in the United States to be married to Taro, a man she has never met. As was common about a century ago, the marriage was arranged by the two young people's families. From that information, write down **what you know** and **what you want to know**. Then read the passage and complete the section in the chart for **what you learn**.

> He quickly made arrangements to have her baggage sent to Oakland, then led her carefully along the rain-slick pier toward the streetcar that would take them to the ferry.
>
> Hana shuddered at the sight of another boat, and as they climbed to its upper deck she felt a queasy tightening of her stomach.
>
> "I hope it will not rock too much," she said anxiously. "Is it many hours to your city?"
>
> Taro laughed for the first time since their meeting, revealing the gold fillings of his teeth. "Oakland is just across the bay," he explained. "We will be there in twenty minutes."
>
> Raising a hand to cover her mouth, Hana laughed with him and suddenly felt better. I am in America now, she thought, and this is the man I came to marry. Then she sat down carefully beside Taro, so no part of their clothing touched.

K What you **Know**	W What you **Want to Know**	L What you **Learn**

DISTINGUISH BETWEEN IMPORTANT AND UNIMPORTANT INFORMATION

Introduction

Writers use a variety of details to discuss a topic or tell a story, and some details may be more important than others. By learning to distinguish between important and unimportant information, readers can focus on what is worth remembering. Study the following steps that a reader can take to distinguish between important and unimportant information.

5. Explain why this information is important or unimportant.
4. Ask yourself, "Should I remember this information?"
3. Identify the details the writer gives.
2. Decide what the passage is about.
1. Read the whole passage.

Model

Use the steps to help you identify the important and less important information in this passage from "Susan Butcher and the Iditarod Trail" by Ellen M. Dolan. Compare your answers to the ones below.

> In January, in the year 1925, the "Black Death" struck two children in Nome, a gold-rush town on the northwest coast of Alaska. "Black Death" was the northern name for diphtheria, a deadly disease. Its name alone terrified parents, for it was often young children who were infected. Symptoms of the disease were a sore throat and fever. These could quickly lead to rapid heartbeat, difficult breathing, choking, and soon…death.
>
> Curtis Welch was the only doctor in Nome, but fortunately he was a good one. Dr. Welch had seen no signs of the "Black Death" for many years. Now he recognized its telltale white spots in the children's throats and knew it was back. Diphtheria spread quickly. More than fifteen hundred people, many of them children, were at risk.

Important Information

- "Black Death" is a name for diphtheria, a deadly disease.
- Dr. Welch knew that more than fifteen hundred people, including many children, were at risk in January, 1925. These ideas are important because they reveal the conflict in the story.

Less Important Information

- Nome was a gold-rush town in northwestern Alaska.
- Dr. Welch was the only doctor in Nome.

These details do not help the reader understand the conflict.

NAME _______________________________   DATE _____________

Practice

Part I

Read the passage below from "Susan Butcher and the Iditarod Trail."
Then, fill in the chart.

> At last doctors from a hospital in Anchorage, Alaska, almost one thousand miles southeast, answered. They found 300,000 units of the serum among their supplies. It was, however, the middle of winter in the frigid North. How should they ship the serum?
>
> This was a difficult problem. There were three ways to get from Anchorage to Nome: by sea, by air, or by combined train/dog sled on land. Winter in Nome was so cold that the Bering sea froze in rippling waves of ice. So no ship could get up the coast from Anchorage to Nome until the spring thaw. The second choice, by air, was risky. There were only two small single-engine biplanes near Fairbanks, Alaska, but they had been dismantled and stored for the winter. The third choice was a three-hundred-mile journey by train from Anchorage to Nenana, a town near Fairbanks, and then a six-or seven-hundred-mile sled-dog drive along a U.S. mail and supply route through the desolate, forbidding country in the Alaskan interior.

What is the passage about?		
What details are given?	**Should I remember this information?**	**Why or why not?**

NAME _______________________________ **DATE** _______________

Part II

Read the following passage from an article about otters written by Joseph A. Davis for *The World Book Encyclopedia*. If you were preparing a report about the physical characteristics and the behavior of otters, which information from this article would you include? Which information would you not include? At the bottom of this page, note the information that would be less important for your report. Explain why you would not include it. Then, fill in the map on the next page.

Otter is a member of the weasel family. Otters live close to water and spend much time in it. Otters live on all the continents except Australia and Antarctica. Most otters weigh from 10 to 30 pounds (4.5 to 14 kilograms) and grow from 3 to 4 ½ feet (0.9 to 1.4 meters) long, including the tail.

Body. An otter has a small flattened head; a long, thick neck; and a thick tail that narrows to a point. Special muscles enable the animal to close its ears and nostrils tightly to keep water out. Elastic webbing grows between the otter's toes. In most species, the webbing is extensive enough to help the animals swim swiftly. Otters, like beavers and muskrats, have long coarse *guard hairs* that cover and protect the short, thick underfur.

Otters often use their paws to handle objects. They hold and play skillfully with such things as stones and small shellfish. Otters spend much time playing. They wrestle and romp and slide down steep muddy slopes in summer and down icy riverbanks in winter. Otters use a variety of sounds to communicate among themselves. All species have a warning growl. Most otters make their homes in burrows in riverbanks or under rocky ledges, or in abandoned dens of other animals. People hunt otters for their valuable and beautiful fur. Certain species, especially the giant otter, are in danger of becoming extinct.

Scientific classification. Otters belong to the weasel family, Mustelidae. The North American otter is *Lutra canadensis*. The giant otter is *Pteronura brasiliensis*. The clawless and small-clawed otters form genus *Aonyx*. The clawless otter is classified *A. capensis*.

Less important information:

1. ____
2. ____
3. ____
4. ____

Why?

1. ____
2. ____
3. ____

Part III

Fill in the center circle with your topic and the outer circles with subtopics. Write important details on the lines. Explain your choices.

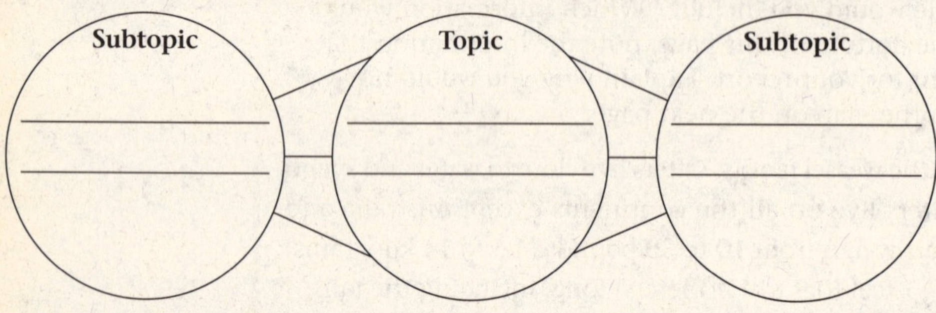

Why I chose these details:

____

____

____

____

____

____

DISTINGUISH BETWEEN FACT AND OPINION OR NONFACT

Introduction

A text may contain facts, nonfacts, and opinions. In order to evaluate what they are reading, readers need to be aware of the distinction between fact and opinion or fact and nonfact.

A **fact** is a statement that can be proved to be true. Ways to prove facts include using reference sources, observation, and prior knowledge.

An **opinion** is the writer's personal feeling or belief. An opinion may not be false, but it cannot be proved to be true.

A **nonfact** is a statement based on guessing. It contains no evidence for proof.

Helpful Hints

Readers can look for certain words or phrases that signal opinions. Examples of these signal words and phrases include the following:

I think	*pretty*	*wonderful*	*terrible*
probably	*ugly*	*safe*	*dangerous*

Model

The following paragraph from "Brown vs. Board of Education" by Walter Dean Myers contains statements that express facts and opinions.

> At Howard there was a law professor, Charles Hamilton Houston, who would affect the lives of many African-American lawyers and who would influence the legal aspects of the civil rights movement. Houston was a great teacher, one who demanded that his students be not just good lawyers but great lawyers. If they were going to help their people—and for Houston the only reason to become lawyers was to do just that—they would have to have absolute understanding of the law, and be diligent in the preparation of their cases. At the time, Houston was an attorney for the N.A.A.C.P. and fought against discrimination in housing and in jobs.

Facts	Opinion
Houston was a law professor at Howard.	Houston was a great teacher.
Houston was demanding of his students.	He influenced the civil rights movement.
He was an attorney for the N.A.A.C.P.	He thought that the only reason to become a lawyer was to help one's people.

Decide whether the statement below is fact, nonfact, or opinion.

For a lawyer, good preparation is less important than good luck. You're right if you decided that the statement is nonfact. This statement is based on pure guesswork. There is no evidence to support it, and it may be proved to be untrue.

NAME ____ **DATE** ___________

Practice

Part I

Below is a passage from "Achieving the American Dream" by Mario Cuomo. Read the passage and decide which statements are facts and which are opinions. Fill in the chart.

> From my earliest days, I felt immersed in the culture and traditions of my parents' homeland. I grew up speaking Italian. I heard story after story from my parents and relatives about life in the Old Country.
>
> Though not an immigrant myself, I saw the hardships Italian immigrants had to endure. I saw their struggle to make themselves understood in an alien language, their struggle to rise out of poverty, and their struggle to overcome the prejudices of people who felt superior because they or their ancestors had arrived earlier on this nation's shores.
>
> As an Italian American, I grew up believing that America is the greatest country on earth, and thankful that I was born here. But at the same time, I have always been intensely proud that I am the son of Italian immigrants and that my Italian heritage helped make me the man I am.

Statement or Idea	Fact?	Opinion?	Why?

NAME _______________________________________ **DATE** _____________

Part II

The following passage is taken from "The Man Without a Country" by
Edward Everett Hale. Read the passage and look for facts and nonfacts.
Answer the questions.

> I suppose that very few casual readers of the *New York Herald* of August 13,
> 1863, observed, in an obscure corner, among the "Deaths,"the announce-
> ment:
>
> NOLAN. Died, on board U.S. Corvette *Levant*, Lat. 2° 11' S., Long. 131°
> W., on the 11th of May, PHILIP NOLAN.
>
> Hundreds of readers would have paused at the announcement had it
> read thus: "Died, May 11, THE MAN WITHOUT A COUNTRY." For it was
> as "the Man Without a Country" that poor Philip Nolan had generally
> been known by the officers who had him in charge during some fifty
> years, as, indeed, by all the men who sailed under them.
>
> There can now be no possible harm in telling this poor creature's story.
> Reason enough there has been till now for very strict secrecy, the secrecy
> of honor itself, among the gentlemen of the Navy who have had Nolan
> in charge….

1. What facts can you find in this passage? How can they be proved?

   ____

   ____

   ____

   ____

   ____

2. What nonfacts can you find in this passage? How do you know?

   ____

   ____

   ____

   ____

   ____

   ____

NAME ____ **DATE** ______________

Part III

Read the passage below from "Exploring the Titanic" by Robert D. Ballard. Identify at least one fact, one opinion, and one nonfact. Give reasons for your decisions.

> As her name boasted, the *Titanic* was indeed the biggest ship in the world. Nicknamed "the Millionaires' Special," she was also called "the Wonder Ship," "the Unsinkable Ship," and "the Last Word in Luxury" by newspapers around the world.
>
> The command of the great ocean liner was given to the senior captain of the White Star Line, Captain Edward J. Smith. This proud, white-bearded man was a natural leader and was popular with both crew members and passengers. Most important, after thirty- eight years' service with the White Star Line, he had an excellent safety record. At the age of fifty-nine, Captain Smith was going to retire after this last trip, a perfect final tribute to a long and successful career.

Fact: **Reason:**

___________________________   ___________________________

___________________________   ___________________________

___________________________   ___________________________

Opinion: **Reason:**

___________________________   ___________________________

___________________________   ___________________________

___________________________   ___________________________

Nonfact: **Reason:**

___________________________   ___________________________

___________________________   ___________________________

___________________________   ___________________________

NAME ____   DATE _______________

EVALUATE AUTHOR'S PURPOSE AND POINT OF VIEW

Introduction

What different kinds of written materials—newspaper articles, travel brochures, recipes, magazine ads, instruction manuals, stories, postcards, speeches, textbook chapters, or poems—have you read this week? For what purpose was each of these pieces written? An **author's purpose** is the main reason that he or she has for writing.

An author's purpose may be one of the following:

to entertain	to persuade
to describe	to inform

For example, an author's main reason for writing a play or a story is to entertain. A travel brochure about a tropical island is written to describe, and a letter to the editor is written to persuade. An author's purpose in writing an encyclopedia article is to inform. Being able to recognize why an author wrote a particular piece will help you to determine how you will read it and to appreciate what you read better.

The perspective an author takes when writing is called **point of view**. When you read nonfiction, or factual writing about real people, places, and events, the author's point of view is his or her opinions or attitudes toward a subject. By reading a selection carefully and by noting details, you can draw conclusions about an author's ideas and feelings.

When you read fiction, or writing about imaginary people, places, and events, the story is told from the point of view of an imaginary character. An author may tell a story from first-person or third-person point of view. The chart below shows the differences between these points of view.

First Person	Third Person
A character in the story tells what happens, using the pronouns *I*, *me*, and *we*.	A narrator who is not one of the characters in the story tells what happens, using the pronouns *he*, *she*, and *it*.

NAME _______________________________   **DATE** _____________

Practice

A. Read the passage below from "Last Cover," a short story by Paul
Annixter. Then complete the sentences that follow.

I'm not sure I can tell you what you want to know about my brother; but
everything about the pet fox is important, so I'll tell all that from the
beginning.

It goes back to a winter afternoon after I'd hunted the woods all day
for a sign of our lost pet. I remember the way my mother looked up as I
came into the kitchen. Without my speaking, she knew what had
happened. For six hours I had walked, reading signs, looking for a delicate
print in the damp soil or even a hair that might have told of a red fox
passing that way—but I had found nothing.

"Did you go up in the foothills?" Mom asked.

I nodded. My face was stiff from held-back tears. My brother, Colin,
who was going on twelve, got it all from one look at me and went into
a heartbroken, almost silent, crying.

Three weeks before, Bandit, the pet fox Colin and I had raised from a
tiny kit, had disappeared, and not even a rumor had been heard of him since.

1. The author's purpose is ____

   ____

2. The point of view is ____

   ____

B. Challenge!
Complete the chart below. List three different works of fiction or
nonfiction that you have recently read. Then identify the author's
purpose and point of view.

What I Have Read	Author's Purpose	Point of View

DRAW CONCLUSIONS

Introduction

Drawing conclusions means making judgments about what has
happened or what you have learned in your reading. Writers usually lead
the reader to a conclusion by arranging their facts in an orderly way.
When you read, use a diagram like the following to keep track of the
facts and the conclusions you can draw from them.

> **Supporting Facts**
>
> ______________________________________
>
> ______________________________________
>
> **Conclusion**
>
> ______________________________________
>
> ______________________________________

Model

What conclusions can you draw from the supporting facts in this passage
from "Debbie" by James Herriot? Compare your answers to the ones below.

> Mrs. Ainsworth was a plumpish, pleasant-faced woman in her forties and
> the kind of client veterinary surgeons dream of: well off, generous, and
> the owner of three cosseted[1] Basset hounds. And it only needed the habit-
> ually mournful expression of one of the dogs to deepen a little and I was
> round there posthaste.[2] Today one of the Bassets had raised its paw and
> scratched its ear a couple of times and that was enough to send its mistress
> scurrying to the phone in great alarm.
>
> So my visits to the Ainsworth home were frequent but undemanding,
> and I had ample opportunity to look out for the little cat that had intrigued
> me. On one occasion I spotted her nibbling daintily from a saucer at the
> kitchen door. As I watched she turned and almost floated on light footsteps
> into the hall....
>
> ______________
> 1. **cosseted:** Pampered; indulged.
> 2. **posthaste:** With great speed.

1. Supporting Facts: Mrs. Ainsworth pampers her Basset hounds. She
   calls the veterinarian at the drop of a hat.
   Conclusion: Mrs. Ainsworth is very anxious about her dogs' health.
2. Supporting Facts: Herriot says the cat intrigued him. He notices the
   cat eating daintily from a saucer.
   Conclusion: Herriot is very curious about the little cat.

Practice

Part I

This passage from "Debbie" by James Herriot is followed by three conclusions. List the supporting facts above the conclusions that are correct and cross out the conclusions that are wrong.

> To the Bassets, Buster's arrival was rather like the intrusion of an irreverent outsider into an exclusive London club. For a long time they had led a life of measured grace; regular sedate walks with their mistress, superb food in ample quantities and long snoring sessions on the rugs and armchairs. Their days followed one upon another in unruffled calm. And then came Buster.
>
> He was dancing up to the youngest dog again, sideways this time, head on one side, goading him. When he started boxing with both paws it was too much even for the Basset. He dropped his dignity and rolled over with the cat in a brief wrestling match.

1. Supporting Facts: ____

____

Conclusion: The dogs enjoyed a calm life of ease before Buster's arrival.

2. Supporting Facts: ____

____

Conclusion: Buster was a playful cat.

3. Supporting Facts: ____

____

Conclusion: Buster was not well treated by Mrs. Ainsworth.

Part II

Below is a passage from "The Trouble with Television," an essay by Robert MacNeil. Read the passage and then answer the questions that follow.

> I believe that TV's appeal to the short attention span is not only inefficient communication but decivilizing as well. Consider the casual assumptions that television tends to cultivate: that complexity must be avoided, that visual stimulation is a substitute for thought, that verbal precision is an anachronism.[9] It may be old-fashioned, but I was taught that thought is words, arranged in grammatically precise ways.
>
> There is a crisis of literacy in this country. One study estimates that some 30 million adult Americans are "functionally illiterate" and cannot read or write well enough to answer a want ad or understand the instructions on a medicine bottle.
>
> Literacy may not be an inalienable human right, but it is one that the highly literate Founding Fathers might not have found unreasonable or even unattainable. We are not only not attaining it as a nation, statistically speaking, but we are falling further and further short of attaining it. And, while I would not be so simplistic as to suggest that television is the cause, I believe it contributes and is an influence.

9. **anachronism:** Anything that seems to be out of its proper place in history.

1. What conclusion can you draw about the writer's outlook or attitude toward television?

   ____

   ____

2. List three facts from this passage that support the conclusion you have drawn.

   a. ____

   ____

   ____

   b. ____

   ____

   ____

   c. ____

   ____

   ____

NAME ______________________________ **DATE** ____________

Part III

Below is a passage from "Charles," a short story by Shirley Jackson. Read the passage and then answer the questions that follow.

> On Saturday I remarked to my husband, "Do you think kindergarten is too unsettling for Laurie? All this toughness, and bad grammar, and this Charles boy sounds like such a bad influence."
>
> "It'll be all right," my husband said reassuringly. "Bound to be people like Charles in the world. Might as well meet them now as later."
>
> On Monday Laurie came home late, full of news. "Charles," he shouted as he came up the hill; I was waiting anxiously on the front steps. "Charles," Laurie yelled all the way up the hill. "Charles was bad again."

Give one conclusion you have drawn from this passage about each of the following characters. Under the conclusion, give one supporting fact that backs it up. The first conclusion is filled in for you.

1. The Narrator
   Conclusion: The narrator is anxious about how her young son is doing at school.

   Supporting Fact: ____

   ____

2. The Narrator's Husband
   Conclusion: ____

   Supporting Fact: ____

   ____

3. Laurie
   Conclusion: ____

   Supporting Fact: ____

   ____

SUMMARIZE

Introduction

To **summarize** means to tell briefly in your own words the main ideas of
a piece of writing. When you summarize, you can condense your ideas or
those of the writer into precise statements and omit unimportant details.
When you are reading, you can choose and remember the most
important parts of the author's writing. When readers write or tell the
"short version" of what they've read, they summarize it. A summary
includes the author's main ideas but leaves out the supporting details.

Model

Read the following passage from "Commodore Perry in the Land of the
Shogun," by Rhoda Blumberg. Find the main idea and supporting details.
Think about how you would summarize this passage, and compare your
ideas to the summary given below.

> Commodore Matthew Calbraith Perry was in command of the squadron.
> He had not come to invade. He hoped to be a peacemaker who would
> make the isolated Empire of Japan a member of "the family of civilized
> nations" of the word. His mission was to unlock Japan's door. It has been
> slammed shut against all but a few Dutch and Chinese traders, the only
> ones officially allowed in for over 200 years.
>
> Perry expected to deliver a letter from President Millard Fillmore to
> the Emperor of Japan….The letter requested that ports be opened so that
> American ships could obtain coal and provisions.
>
> America had invested seventeen million dollars in the Pacific whaling
> industry, and it needed Japanese ports to replenish coal and provisions
> for the whalers. Whale oil was essential for lighting and for lubricating
> machinery.

Here is a *summary* of the same passage:
  Commodore Perry wanted to help American interests in the Pacific by
reopening Japan to trade with the United States.

Practice

Read the following paragraph from *I Know Why the Caged Bird Sings* by Maya Angelou. Then, answer the questions that follow.

> Until I was thirteen and left Arkansas for good, the Store was my favorite place to be. Alone and empty in the mornings, it looked like an unopened present from a stranger. Opening the front doors was pulling the ribbon off the unexpected gift. The light would come in softly (we faced north), easing itself over the shelves of mackerel, salmon, tobacco, thread. It fell flat on the big vat of lard and by noontime during the summer the grease had softened to a thick soup. Whenever I walked into the Store in the afternoon, I sensed that it was tired. I alone could hear the slow pulse of its job half done. But just before bedtime, after numerous people had walked in and out, had argued over their bills, or joked about their neighbors, or just dropped in "to give Sister Henderson a 'Hi y'all,'" the promise of magic mornings returned to the Store and spread itself over the family in washed life waves....

1. What is the main idea of this paragraph?

   ____

2. Name three details that give more information about the main idea.

   ____

   ____

3. Use a complete sentence or sentences to summarize the paragraph.

   ____

   ____

4. **Challenge!**
   Read the following paragraph from *I Know Why the Caged Bird Sings* by Maya Angelou. Then, write a summary in one or two sentences.

> As I ate [Mrs. Flowers] began the first of what we later called "my lessons in living." She said that I must always be intolerant of ignorance but understanding of illiteracy. That some people, unable to go to school, were more educated and even more intelligent than college professors. She encouraged me to listen carefully to what country people called mother wit. That in those homely sayings was couched the collective wisdom of generations.

Summary

____

____

____

PARAPHRASE

Introduction

When you use your own words to repeat someone else's message, you **paraphrase** what they have said. Paraphrasing is a helpful reading tool. When you are reading, identify the main ideas and their supporting details. If you can tell a story accurately in your own words, it shows that you understand the meaning of what you have read. Unlike a summary, where the reader is concerned mostly with the author's main ideas, a paraphrase also includes details.

Model

Read this passage from "E-Mail from Bill Gates" by John Seabrook. Paraphrase it in your mind as you read it. Compare your paraphrase with the one below.

> At the moment, the best way to communicate with another person on the information highway[1] is to exchange electronic mail: to write a message on a computer and send it through the telephone lines into someone else's computer. In the future, people will send each other sound and pictures as well as text, and do it in real time,[2] and improved technology will make it possible to have rich, human electronic exchanges, but at present E-mail is the closest thing we have to that. Even now, E-mail allows you to meet and communicate with people in a way that would be impossible on the phone, through the regular mail, or face to face, as I discovered while I was working on this story.

1. **information highway:** Network of computers and file servers that allows for the rapid exchange of electronic information.
2. **real time:** Accessing of information or exchange of data that requires no downloading of files.

Paraphrased Version

The best way to communicate now by computer is through electronic mail. In the future, it will be possible to send sound and pictures as well as text. Even now, E-mail allows people to communicate with each other in a unique way.

NAME _________________________________ **DATE** _________

Practice

Paraphrase the following passage from "Christmas Day in the Morning"
by Pearl Buck.

> He woke suddenly and completely. It was four o'clock, the hour at which
> his father had always called him to get up and help with the milking.
> Strange how the habits of his youth clung to him still! Fifty years ago,
> and his father had been dead for thirty years, and yet he waked at four
> o'clock in the morning. He had trained himself to turn over and go to
> sleep, but this morning, because it was Christmas, he did not try to sleep.
>
> Yet what was the magic of Christmas now? His childhood and youth
> were long past, and his own children had grown up and gone. Some of
> them lived only a few miles away but they had their own families, and
> though they would come in as usual toward the end of the day, they had
> explained with infinite gentleness that they wanted their children to
> build Christmas memories about *their* houses, not his. He was left alone
> with his wife.

____

____

____

____

____

____

____

____

____

NAME ___________________________________ **DATE** ___________

FORM GENERALIZATIONS

Introduction

Effective readers sometimes act as detectives. They look for specific clues in their reading material and put these clues together to solve the mystery of the larger meaning of what they have read. When readers do this, they form **generalizations**, or broad ideas on what might be true in the book, story, or passage.

To form generalizations as you read, look carefully for sentences that relate to each other. Then ask yourself if the sentences give you general information that might be true but is not directly stated. If so, you have formed a generalization.

Model

Read the following passage from "Why Leaves Turn Color in the Fall" by Diane Ackerman. As you read, try to form one or more generalizations about the information in the passage. See if your generalizations agree with the example given below.

> The most spectacular range of fall foliage occurs in the northeastern United States and in eastern China, where the leaves are robustly colored thanks in part to a rich climate. European maples don't achieve the same flaming red as their American relatives, which thrive on cold nights and sunny days. In Europe, the warm, humid weather turns the leaves brown or mildly yellow.

Generalization

Fall leaves are most brilliant in two regions of the world: the northeastern United States and eastern China.

This sentence states the central idea of the paragraph.

Supporting information from the passage

Climate affects leaf color. European maples do not achieve the same color as American maples.
For rich color change, maples thrive on cold nights and sunny days.
The weather in Europe is warm and humid.

This supporting information helps to illustrate the generalization.

Practice

Read these two passages from "Why Leaves Turn Color in the Fall" by Diane Ackerman. Make at least one generalization about each passage, and support it with information found there.

> Not all leaves turn the same color. Elms, weeping willows, and the ancient gingko all grow radiant yellow, along with hickories, aspens, bottlebrush buckeyes, cottonweeds, and tall, keening poplars. Basswood turns bronze, birches bright gold. Water-loving maples put on a symphonic display of scarlets. Sumacs turn red, too, as do flowering dogwoods, black gums, and sweet gums. Though some oaks yellow, most turn a pinkish brown. The farmlands also change color, as tepees of cornstalks and bales of shredded-wheat-textured hay stand drying in the fields. In some spots, one slope of a hill may be green and the other already in bright color, because the hillside facing south gets more sun and heat than the northern one.

1. Generalization(s)

____

____

2. Supporting Information

____

____

> We call the season "fall," from the Old English *feallen*, to fall, which leads back through time to the Indo-European *phol*, which also means to fall. So the word and the idea are both extremely ancient, and haven't really changed since the first of our kind needed a name for fall's leafy abundance. As we say the word, we're reminded of that other Fall, in the Garden of Eden, when fig leaves never withered and scales fell from our eyes. Fall is the time when leaves fall from the trees, just as spring is when flowers spring up, summer is when we simmer, and winter is when we whine from the cold.

1. Generalization(s)

____

____

2. Supporting Information

____

____

NAME ____   DATE _____________

Read the following passage. Then, answer the questions that follow. Write the letter of the correct answer on the line at the right.

> After the meeting I identified and sought out Laurie's kindergarten teacher. She had a plate with a cup of tea and a piece of chocolate cake; I had a plate with a cup of tea and a piece of marshmallow cake. We maneuvered up to one another cautiously, and smiled.

[Shirley Jackson, "Charles"]

1. Which word rhymes with the word *sought*?   1. ______
   A. rough   B. enough   C. dough   D. taut

2. How should the word *marshmallow* be divided into syllables?   2. ______
   A. marsh-mal-low   C. marsh-mallow
   B. mar-shmal-low   D. marsh-mall-ow

Read the following passage. Then, answer the questions that follow. Write the letter of the correct answer on the line at the right.

> And then on the night before Christmas, that year when he was fifteen, he lay for a few minutes thinking about the next day. They were poor, and most of the excitement was in the turkey they had raised themselves and in the mince pies his mother made. His sisters sewed presents and his mother and father always bought something he needed, not only a warm jacket, maybe, but something more, such as a book. And he saved and bought them each something, too.

[Pearl Buck, "Christmas Day in the Morning"]

3. Which item below best describes the author's purpose and point of view?   3. ______
   A. to entertain; first person
   B. to entertain; third person
   C. to inform; third person
   D. to persuade; first person

4. From the details in the passage, you can reliably infer that   4. ______
   A. the character grew up in a close-knit, loving family
   B. the character felt like an outsider when he was young
   C. the family did not regard the holiday as important
   D. the family's poverty was a cause of unhappiness

NAME ____   **DATE** ______________

Read the following passage. Then, answer the questions that follow. Write the letter of the correct answer on the line at the right.

> The grandfather had become very old. His legs would not carry him, his eyes could not see, his ears could not hear, and he was toothless. When he ate, bits of food sometimes dropped out of his mouth. His son and his son's wife no longer allowed him to eat with them at the table. He had to eat his meals in the corner near the stove.

[Leo Tolstoy, "The Old Grandfather and His Little Grandson"]

5. Which statement best expresses the main idea of the passage?   5. ______
   A. The stove was in the corner of the room.
   B. The grandfather had become very old.
   C. The grandfather had difficulty chewing his food.
   D. The son was married.

6. Which word below rhymes with *could*?   6. ______
   A. hood   B. cold   C. cud   D. cod

Read the following passage. Then, answer the questions that follow. Write the letter of the correct answer on the line at the right.

> There are half a dozen meteor showers each year. Each is named after the constellation from which it appears to come. The biggest of all, the Perseids, named for the constellation of Perseus, occurs on the 10th, 11th, and 12th of August. The next largest, the Leonids, named for the constellation of Leo, comes on the nights of November 14, 15, and 16. Another, the Andromedids, which is not quite so big, comes from November 17 through 23. There are other meteor showers in December, January, April, May, and July, but none of them is as big as those in August and November.

[Hal Borland, "Shooting Stars"]

7. According to the passage, which meteor showers occur in the month of   7. ______
   November?
   A. the Leonids but not the Andromedids
   B. the Perseids but not the Leonids
   C. both the Perseids and the Leonids
   D. both the Leonids and the Andromedids

8. Which of the following statements best summarizes the passage?   8. ______
   A. Of the half dozen meteor showers in a year, the biggest are the Perseids,
      the Leonids, and the Andromedids.
   B. Meteor showers are named after the constellations from which they
      appear to come.
   C. The Leonids occur in November, but the Perseids occur in August.
   D. The Andromedids shower occurs late in the year.

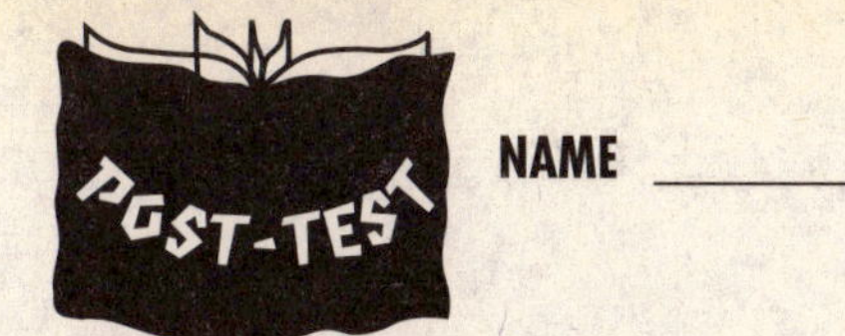

9. How are the Andromedids different from the Leonids?   9. _____
    A. They occur in different months.
    B. The Andromedids shower is not named for a constellation.
    C. The Andromedids shower is not quite so big as the Leonids.
    D. The Andromedids shower does not last as many days as the Leonids does.

Read the following passage. Then, answer the questions that follow. Write the letter of the correct answer on the line at the right.

> Each step became more difficult and perilous, and he was faint from exertion and from lack of Swanson's dinner. Three or four times he slipped slightly and recovered himself; but, growing careless from exhaustion and the long tension on his nerves, he tried to continue with too great haste, and was rewarded by a double slip of each foot, which tore him loose and started him down the slope.

[Jack London, "Up the Slide"]

10. From context clues in the passage, how would you define *exertion*?   10. _____
    A. exercise   **C.** energetic effort
    B. extreme cold   **D.** perspiration

11. The word *perilous* contains the root *peril*. Which word below best defines the   11. _____
    meaning of *perilous*?
    A. rapid   **B.** dangerous   **C.** smooth   **D.** challenging

12. What does the suffix *-ly* mean in *slightly*?   12. _____
    A. state, quality   **C.** in the manner of
    B. action, process   **D.** the most

Read the following passage. Then, answer the questions that follow. Write the letter of the correct answer on the line at the right.

> Every part of this earth is sacred to my people. Every shining pine needle, every sandy shore, every mist in the dark woods, every meadow, every humming insect. All are holy in the memory and experience of my people. We know the sap which courses through the trees as we know the blood that courses through our veins.

[Chief Seattle, "This We Know"]

13. Which statement below best expresses the main idea of the passage?   13. _____
    A. There are many different sides to nature on the earth.
    B. Every part of this earth is sacred to my people.
    C. Some of my people respect nature, but others do not.
    D. We cannot live if we are forced to move from our homeland.

14. From context clues in the passage, how would you define the verb *courses*?   14. _____
    A. blocks   **B.** runs   **C.** stops   **D.** connects

15. How should the word *experience* be divided into syllables?   15. ______
  A. ex-per-i-ence   **C.** exper-i-ence
  B. ex-pe-ri-en-ce   **D.** e-xper-i-ence

Read the following passage. Then, answer the questions that follow. Write the
letter of the correct answer on the line at the right.

> It took months of negotiation to come to an understanding with the old man.
> He was in no hurry. What he had the most was time. He lived up in Río en
> Medio, where his people had been for hundreds of years. He tilled the same land
> they had tilled. His house was small and wretched, but quaint. The little creek
> ran through his land. His orchard was gnarled and beautiful.

[Juan R. R. Sedillo, "Gentleman of Río en Medio"]

16. Which of the following states a *fact* in the passage?   16. ______
  A. The old man's house was wretched but quaint.
  B. The orchard was beautiful.
  C. The old man seemed honest.
  D. It took months to reach an agreement with the old man.

17. Which of the following states an *opinion* from the passage?   17. ______
  A. The old man's house was wretched, but quaint.
  B. The old man lived in Río en Medio.
  C. A little creek ran through the old man's land.
  D. The old man's relatives had lived in the same area for hundreds of years.

18. Which statement is the best paraphrase of the first sentence in the passage?   18. ______
  A. The old man did not understand how to negotiate.
  B. It took months to reach an agreement with the old man.
  C. The negotiations with the old man were difficult.
  D. The old man refused for several months to negotiate.

Read the following passage. Then, answer the questions that follow. Write the
letter of the correct answer on the line at the right.

> In one meeting with the Board of Health, the developer arose and announced,
> "I'm not going to argue hydro-geological[5] facts with a thirteen-year-old!" Andy's
> parents were angry, but Andy just shrugged his shoulders. Nine months after
> the first meeting, an important test called a "deep-hole test" was conducted in
> the swamp. The purpose of the test was to find out how quickly a hole dug in
> the swamp would fill up with water. If it filled up very fast, that would be a sign
> that the land was not suitable for building.
>
> The developer, members of the Concord Neighborhood Association, and state
> environmental officials gathered to observe the test. The hole was dug—and it
> filled with water almost immediately. Andy grinned clear around his head.

5. **hydro-geological:** Related to water and to the science of the nature and history of the Earth.

[Barbara A. Lewis, "Saving the Wetlands"]

19. Some information in the passage above is important and some is not important. Which information is unimportant?

    A. Andy shrugged his shoulders after the developer spoke.
    B. A deep-hole test was conducted in the swamp.
    C. Observers of the test included the developer, members of the neighborhood association, and state officials.
    D. When the hole was dug, it filled with water almost immediately.

19. ______

20. Which inference below can you reliably make from this passage?

    A. Andy did not get along with his parents.
    B. Andy opposed the development of the swamp.
    C. Andy was unsure of his hydro-geological facts.
    D. The deep-hole test was not conducted properly.

20. ______

21. Which statement below is the best summary of the second paragraph in the passage?

    A. The state officials did not schedule the test until nine months after the first meeting.
    B. Because they are expensive, deep-hole tests are not used very often.
    C. If a hole fills up quickly with water in the deep-hole test, the land is not suitable for building.
    D. Andy knew the results of the deep-hole test would support his position.

21. ______

Read the following passage. Then, answer the questions that follow. Write the letter of the correct answer on the line at the right.

> The twenty-yard dash takes all of two minutes cause most of the little kids don't know no better than to run off the track or run the wrong way or run smack into the fence and fall down and cry. One little kid, though, has got the good sense to run straight for the white ribbon up ahead, so he wins. Then the second-graders line up for the thirty-yard dash and I don't even bother to turn my head to watch cause Raphael Perez always wins. He wins before he even begins by psyching[7] the runners, telling them they're going to trip on their shoelaces and fall on their faces or lose their shorts or something, which he doesn't really have to do since he is very fast, almost as fast as I am. After that is the forty-yard dash which I use to run when I was in first grade.

7. **psyching**: Slang for playing on a person's mental state.

[Toni Cade Bambara, "Raymond's Run"]

22. Which word sounds exactly like the first syllable in *psyching*?

    A. pie   **B.** say   **C.** sigh   **D.** shy

22. ______

23. When does Raphael Perez run his race?

    A. after the twenty-yard dash
    B. before the thirty-yard dash
    C. together with the narrator
    D. together with the first-graders

23. ______

Read the following passage. Then, answer the questions that follow. Write the letter of the correct answer on the line at the right.

> What would the memorial be? What should it look like? Who would design it? Scruggs, Doubek, and Wheeler didn't know, but they were determined that the memorial should help bring closer together a nation still bitterly divided by the Vietnam War. It couldn't be something like the Marine Corps Memorial showing American troops planting a flag on enemy soil at Iwo Jima. It couldn't be a giant dove with an olive branch of peace in its beak. It had to soothe passions, not stir them up. But there was one thing Jan Scruggs insisted on: The memorial, whatever it turned out to be, would have to show the name of every man and woman killed or missing in the war.

[Brent Ashabranner, "Always to Remember: The Vision of Maya Ying Lin"]

24. Which statement below best expresses the contrast that is emphasized in the passage?
    A. Scruggs, Doubek, and Wheeler didn't know who would design the memorial.
    B. The Marine Corps planted a flag on enemy soil at Iwo Jima.
    C. A dove carries an olive branch to symbolize peace.
    D. It had to soothe passions, not stir them up.

24. ______

25. Which conclusion below can you draw from the passage?
    A. The symbolism of the dove and the olive branch would be confusing to viewers.
    B. The most important element in the design for the memorial was the inclusion of all the names.
    C. Scruggs, Doubek, and Wheeler devoted too little time to planning the memorial.
    D. A design competition was not necessary for the building of the memorial.

25. ______

26. The word *memorial* contains the Latin root *mem*. This root appears in all the words below except
    A. commemorate   B. remember   C. memory   D. membership

26. ______

NAME _______________________________   **DATE** _____________

Read the following passage. Then, answer the questions that follow. Write the letter of the correct answer on the line at the right.

> In 1960, my mother bought a television set, and each day after school I watched Hamilton Holmes and Charlayne Hunter[2] as they struggled to integrate—fair-skinned as they were—the University of Georgia. And then, one day, there appeared the face of Dr. Martin Luther King, Jr. What a funny name, I thought. At the moment I first saw him, he was being handcuffed and shoved into a police truck. He had dared to claim his rights as a native son, and had been arrested. He displayed no fear, but seemed calm and serene, unaware of his own extraordinary courage. His whole body, like his conscience, was at peace.
>
> 2 **Hamilton Holmes and Charlayne Hunter:** Hamilton Holmes and Charlayne Hunter made history in January 1961 by becoming the first two African Americans to attend the University of Georgia.

[Alice Walker, "Choice: A Tribute to Dr. Martin Luther King, Jr."]

27. On the basis of this passage, what generalization can you make?   27. _______
    A. The writer wanted to attend the University of Georgia.
    B. Dr. Martin Luther King, Jr., was a man of great courage.
    C. The writer paid little attention to the Civil Rights Movement at that time.
    D. Dr. King was more effective in the struggle for civil rights than Hamilton Holmes and Charlayne Hunter were.

28. Which statement below best expresses the implied main idea of the passage?   28. _______
    A. The author learned about the struggle for civil rights by watching television after school.
    B. Starting in 1961, the University of Georgia began to admit African American students.
    C. The writer's mother had great influence on the writer's opinions.
    D. Dr. Martin Luther King, Jr., was a calm and courageous leader in the struggle for civil rights.

Read the following passage. Then, answer the questions that follow. Write the letter of the correct answer on the line at the right.

> That was when she finally told us that she was working as a check-out clerk at the A&P. She was supposed to be on the day shift, but the other employees were unreliable, and her boss had promised her a promotion if she would stay until the evening shift filled in.
>
>   For a moment no one said anything. Even Mona seemed to find the revelation disappointing.

[Gish Jen, "The White Umbrella"]

29. What does the prefix *un-* mean in *unreliable*?   29. ______
    A. before   **B.** again   **C.** opposite of   **D.** completely

30. Pronounce each word below, paying special attention to the final syllable.   30. ______
    In which word does the final syllable not rhyme with the last syllable
    of *promotion*?
    A. revelation   **B.** exception   **C.** intention   **D.** vision

Use this bar graph to answer the following questions.

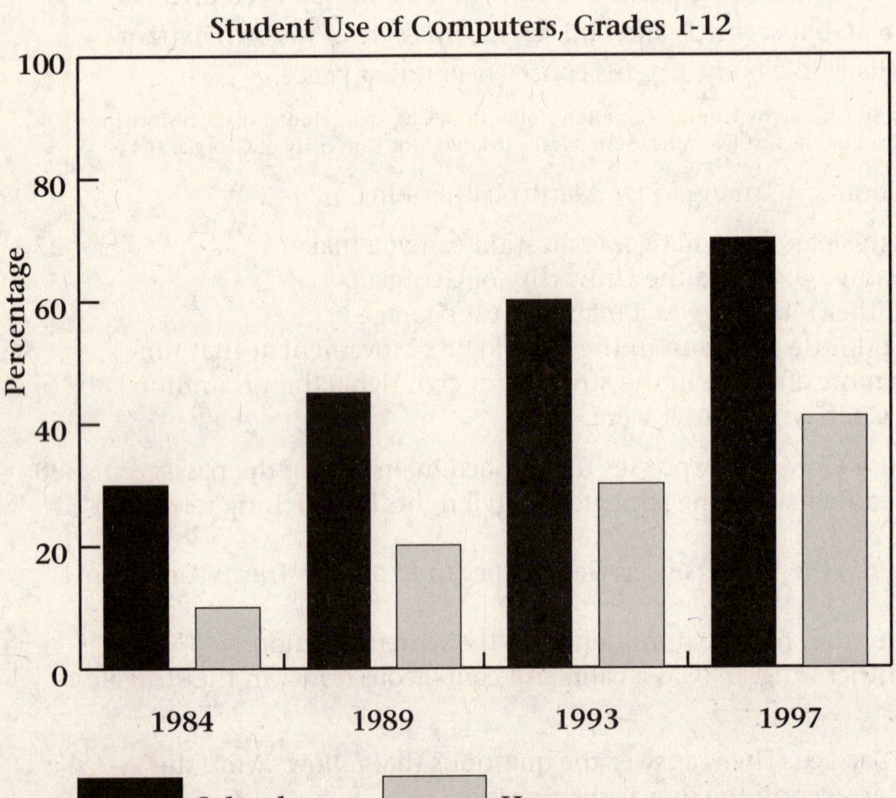

31. According to the graph, when did the percentage of students using computers   31. ______
    at school reach 60%?
    A. 1984   **B.** 1989   **C.** 1993   **D.** 1997

32. Between 1989 and 1997, how much did the percentage of students using   32. ______
    computers at home rise?
    A. from 15% to 30%
    B. from 15% to 41%
    C. from 20% to 41%
    D. from 20% to 25%

Read the following passage. Then, answer the questions that follow. Write the letter of the correct answer on the line at the right.

> Hokusai was born in 1760 outside the city of Edo[2] in the province of Shimofusa. He was apprenticed early in life to a mirror maker and then worked in a lending library, where he was fascinated by the woodcut illustrations of the piled-up books. At eighteen he became a pupil of Shunsho, a great artist known mainly for his prints of actors. Hokusai was soon signing his name as Shunro, and for the next fifteen years he, too, made actor prints, as well as illustrations for popular novels. By 1795 he was calling himself Sori and had begun working with the European copper etchings which had become popular in Japan.

2. **Edo:** Former name of Tokyo.

[Stephen Longstreet, "Hokusai: The Old Man Mad About Drawing"]

33. Which sentence below is the best paraphrase of the second sentence in the passage?
    A. He worked in a mirror maker's shop.
    B. As a youngster, he studied under a mirror maker and then worked in a library, where woodcuts fascinated him.
    C. After he served as an apprentice, he became a librarian.
    D. As a young artist, Hokusai held several jobs.

33. ______

34. When did Hokusai become a pupil of Shunsho?
    A. after he left Edo
    B. before he worked in a lending library
    C. in 1795
    D. when he was eighteen

34. ______

35. One conclusion you can draw from the passage is that
    A. Hokusai had trouble holding a job.
    B. Hokusai had a curious mind and a broad range of interests.
    C. Hokusai quarreled with Shunro.
    D. Hokusai wanted to leave Japan.

35. ______

36. Which item below best describes the author's purpose in this passage?
    A. to entertain   **C.** to persuade
    B. to inform   **D.** to describe

36. ______

NAME ____ DATE _______________

Read the following passage. Then, answer the questions that follow. Write the letter of the correct answer on the line at the right.

> We visited our relative again in the winter. We arrived at night, but first thing in the morning I made straight for the farm and its barn. The shadows under the eaves were too dense to let me spot the sphere from far off. I stepped on the bottom rung of the ladder—slick with frost—and climbed carefully up. My hands and feet kept slipping, so my eyes stayed on the rung ahead, and it was not until I was secure at the top that I could look up. The sphere was gone.
>
> I was crushed. That object had fascinated me like nothing I had come across in my life; I had even grown to love wasps because of it. I sagged on the ladder and watched my breath eddy[7] around the blank eaves. I'm afraid I pitied myself more than the apparently homeless wasps.

7. **eddy:** Move in a circular motion.

[Bruce Brooks, "Animal Craftsmen"]

37. Which word below does not contain a sound that is the same as the sound made by the *ph* in *sphere*?   37. ______
    A. farm   **B.** fascinated   **C.** far   **D.** pitied

38. Which statement below best expresses the implied main idea in the passage?   38. ______
    A. I felt pity for the wasps because they were homeless.
    B. I looked forward greatly to seeing the wasps' home again, but I was bitterly disappointed.
    C. The weather was so cold that I had trouble climbing the ladder in the barn.
    D. I could not understand why the wasps had left their home.

Read the following passage. Then, answer the questions that follow. Write the letter of the correct answer on the line at the right.

> Thus she forced them to go on. Sometimes she thought she had become nothing but a voice speaking in the darkness, cajoling, urging, threatening. Sometimes she told them things to make them laugh, sometimes she sang to them, and heard the eleven voices behind her blending softly with hers, and then she knew that for the moment all was well with them.

[Ann Petry, "Harriet Tubman: Guide to Freedom"]

39. From context clues in the passage, how would you define *cajoling*?   39. ______
    A. shouting   **B.** despairing   **C.** coaxing   **D.** praying

40. On the basis of the passage, what generalization can you make about Harriet Tubman?   40. ______
    A. She was a resourceful, determined leader.
    B. She was persistent but lacked a sense of humor.
    C. She had trouble communicating with the people she was leading.
    D. She always preferred to avoid blunt or angry confrontations.